Utah's Aerospace Heritage

The Aircraft and Artifacts
of
Hill Aerospace Museum

HILL AIR FORCE BASE, UTAH

Edited by
Bob Arnold, Deloy Spencer, Mary Bell Hill, Tom Hill,
Paul F. Anderson, and Mel Broberg

Home Front Historical Publishing

Acknowledgments

The information in this book was updated in 1996 by museum volunteers Smsgt. Charles R. "Bob" Arnold USAF retired, Deloy Spencer, and Col. Jerry Cannon USAF retired. Their seemingly endless hours of labor have been well worth the effort.

Thanks to Deloy Spencer, Paul F. Anderson, and Jim Lawrence for the photography.

A big "Thank You" to Virgie Arnold for countless hours of typing.

Thanks to everyone else who helped put this book together—volunteers, museum staff, museum director, and Foundation members.

Library of Congress Information in Publication Data

ISBN 0-9656079-0-9

Date of publication: December 1996

Published and printed in the USA

Book design and production by Home Front Historical Publishing

ORDERING ADDITIONAL COPIES OF THIS BOOK

Additonal copies of this book may be ordered from:

HILL AEROSPACE MUSEUM GIFT SHOP
P.O. BOX 834
ROY, UT 84067
801-774-0956   FAX 801-775-3034
http://www.hill.af.mil/museum

Published by:
Home Front Historical Publishing
3136 South 3200 West
Salt Lake City, UT 84119

Welcome to Hill Aerospace Museum!

On behalf of the Air Force Heritage Foundation of Utah, I welcome you to Hill Aerospace Museum. We are proud of the museum and its collection, and are pleased to have you as a visitor.

Hill Aerospace Museum is home for nearly sixty military aircraft, some unique and others which are becoming very rare with each passing year. Some of our warbirds have seen action in far-flung areas around the world over the decades. Their service lives may be behind them, but each plane still contains untold memories of heroism and sacrifice. As you stroll the grounds listen closely for the faint echo of powerful engines and the ghostly whispers from pilots of yesteryear. They yearn to tell their stories.

The Air Force Heritage Foundation of Utah offers you this guidebook full of photographs, specifications, and memories as a means of enhancing your visit to Hill Aerospace Museum. We hope you will refer often to this booklet and return frequently to the museum to view a part of history that you may have missed on your previous visit.

The Foundation, a private, non-profit organization, was founded in 1983 with the purpose of raising funds for the establishment and construction of a museum at Hill Air Force Base. Today we continue to provide support for the museum in various ways. We locate and acquire artifacts, including aircraft, for restoration and display. We also work closely with the museum staff to achieve other improvements which help the museum present the history of the United States Air Force in Utah.

Again, we are very pleased that you have joined the ranks of the many friends of Hill Aerospace Museum. We hope you will come back often. Enjoy your visit!

Marc C. Reynolds

Lt. Gen. Marc C. Reynolds (USAF, ret.)

Chairman, Board of Directors

Air Force Heritage Foundation of Utah

Table of Contents

The Mission of the Museum

Our mission at Hill Aerospace Museum is to preserve the heritage and traditions of the United States Air Force by:

- collecting, preserving, and displaying historically significant Air Force artifacts
- depicting the significant role that Hill Air Force Base and the State of Utah have had in Air Force history
- meeting United States Air Force Museum System requirements as defined in Air Force Instruction 84-103
- fostering a neighborly relationship between Hill AFB and its surrounding communities, thereby strengthening Air Force public relations
- providing an educational setting where visitors can learn more about the history, function, and mission of the United States Air Force, its role in our nation's defense, and its airplanes and how they function.

Hill Aerospace Museum

A Short History of Hill Air Force Base

Hill Air Force Base has enjoyed a long and colorful history. The base traces its origins back to the ill-fated Army Air Mail "experiment" of 1934, during which time the idea originated for a permanent air depot in the Salt Lake City area. In the years that followed, the Army Air Corps searched the region for an ideal location for its permanent western terminus. Several sites in Utah were considered, with the present site near Ogden emerging as the clear favorite.

In July 1939 Congress appropriated $8 million for the establishment and construction of the Ogden Air Depot. In December of that year the War Department named the site "Hill Field," in honor of Major Ployer Peter Hill, Chief of the Flying Branch of the Air Corps Materiel Division at Wright Field in Dayton, Ohio. Major Hill had died as a result of injuries received from the crash of the Boeing experimental aircraft Model 299 at Wright Field, the prototype of what would later become the famous B-17 Flying Fortress.

The official groundbreaking ceremonies for Hill Field were held on 12 January 1940, although actual construction of the base had already begun. The first Commander of the Ogden Air Depot, Colonel Morris Berman, arrived at Hill Field on 7 November 1940, marking the beginning of official operations at the field.

During World War II Hill Field was a vital maintenance and supply base, with round-the-clock operations geared to supporting the war effort. Battle weary A-26, B-17, B-24, B-29, P-40, P-47, P-61, and many other types of aircraft depended on the men and women of Hill Field for structural repair, engine overhaul, and spare parts. Peak wartime

During WWII work never ceased at Hill. This 1944 photograph was taken during the swing shift—around-the-clock operations.

WWII propeller shop at Hill (1943-1944)

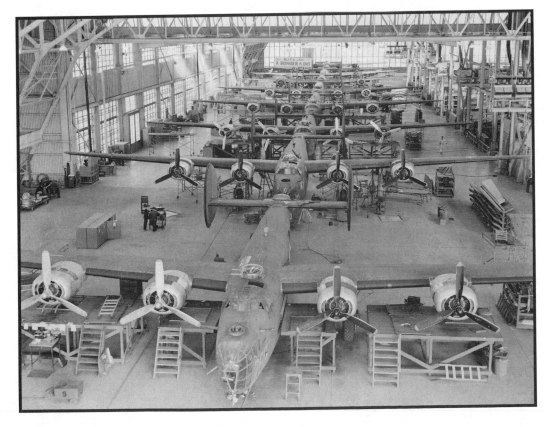

B-24 assembly line at Hill

employment at Hill was reached in 1943 with a total of over 22,000 military and civilian personnel. These dedicated men and women rehabilitated and returned thousands of warbirds to combat.

In 1944 Hill Field became responsible for the long-term storage of surplus aircraft and support equipment. PT-17, B-24, P-40, P-47, B-29, and many other types of aircraft were eventually prepared and stored at the base. By the end of 1947 more than $200 million worth of aircraft had been preserved in near perfect condition for possible future use. During the massive demobilization that followed World War II, Hill Field also reclaimed scores of surplus aircraft, which were disassembled and some parts put back into the supply system.

On 26 September 1947 the Army Air Corps became the United States Air Force, ending an association with the Army that had lasted 40 years. Following an Air Force-wide pattern of renaming "fields" as "bases," Hill Field became Hill Air Force Base on 5 February 1948.

When North Korea invaded South Korea in 1950, Hill AFB was assigned a major share of Project Holdoff, the Air Materiel Command's logistical effort to support the war. Hill personnel quickly removed needed B-26s and B-29s from storage, renovated, and added them to the active Air Force inventory.

Also in the 1950s, the Ogden Air Materiel Area, the ranking activity at Hill, began support of jet aircraft, such as the F-84F Thunderstreak, F-84G Thunderjet, RF-84J Thunderflash, F-89 Scorpion, F/RF-101 Voodoo, F-102 Delta Dagger, B-47 Stratojet, and B-57 Night Intruder. OOAMA also assumed prime maintenance responsibilities for the SM-62 Snark, IM-99 Bomarc, SM-73 Goose, and SM-64 Navaho missile systems, as well as the MB-1 Genie rocket system. OOAMA entered into ballistic missile support with the SM-65 Atlas ICBM in 1958 and the SM-80 Minuteman ICBM in 1959.

In the 1960s, OOAMA was assigned support and system management duties for the USAF F-4 Phantom II, Titan II/Titan III missiles, and the AGM-65A Maverick missile. Hill AFB also supported the war in Southeast Asia by direct

As the sun slowly sets on the Great Salt Lake, activities at Hill Field temporarily come to a halt and the officers pay tribute to Old Glory. In the background a B-25 is being "gassed up" prior to take-off.

Aerial photo of HAFB storage areas

Aerial photo in early 1944

airlifts of hundreds of tons of airmunitions via C-124, C-130, C-133, and C-141 aircraft. The base also picked up maintenance responsibilities for B-58 Hustler and F/RF/FB-111A landing gear components.

Hill began managing certain components of the F-15 Eagle in 1971. That same year field testing began at Hill on the UH-1H Huey helicopter. The following year saw the production of the first version of the Short Range Attack Missile (SRAM), delivered from Boeing Air Force Plant 77 at Hill AFB. The Ogden Air Logistics Center also became system manager of the F-16 Fighting Falcon, the Advanced Intercontinental Ballistic (M-X) Missile System, and the A-10 Thunderbolt II in the 1970s. OOALC had logistics responsibility for Alaska, western Canada, Idaho, Montana, North and South Dakota, Wyoming, Utah, Colorado, Arizona, and New Mexico.

The 1980s saw the assignment of repair responsibilities for the BGM-109G Ground Launched Cruise Missile (GLCM) to Hill. During Fiscal Year 1980 Hill AFB also had the busiest single runway of any airfield in the free world. Airfield traffic totaled 145,243 takeoffs and landings. The OOALC Directorate of Distribution then managed an inventory valued at $2,039,195,215. The base was also assigned repair projects for the OV-10A Bronco and C-130 Hercules aircraft.

In August 1990 OOALC and Hill began support of Operation Desert Shield by helping to sustain the U.S. deployment to Southwest Asia. All shifts and work hours were extended to support the various aircraft involved in the mission. The 388th Tactical Fighter Wing, a Hill tenant, also deployed its 4th and 421st Tactical Fighter Squadrons to Southwest Asia. When Desert Shield became Desert Storm in 1991 Hill AFB personnel at home and abroad continued to support the mission in Southwest Asia. In 1993 Hill was awarded contracts for the modification, corrosion control, and painting of 244 Navy F/A-18 Hornet fighters and the maintenance and repair of landing gear on various USAF, DoD, and allied aircraft.

From modest beginnings, Hill AFB now ranks as Utah's largest employer. The $500 million payroll and presence of the installation injects tremendous growth into the Utah economy. The current value of the base acreage, buildings, equipment, and inventories exceeds $4.5 billion.

Aerial photo of Hill Aerospace Museum construction (1990)

Major Ployer Peter Hill (1894-1935), Namesake of Hill AFB

Ployer Peter ("Pete") Hill was known as an extremely capable and meticulous pilot, and an officer and gentleman of truly great distinction. In an exemplary aviation career that spanned eighteen years, Hill piloted nearly 60 of the Army Air Corps' newest and best aircraft, testing and evaluating their capabilities for service.

Pete Hill was born in Newburyport, Massachusetts on 24 October 1894 and attended grammar school and high school in his hometown. In 1916 he graduated from Brown University with a Bachelor of Science degree in Civil Engineering. The following year he enlisted in the Aviation Section of the U.S. Army Signal Enlisted Reserve Corps. In 1918 he received flight instruction at the School of Military Aeronautics at Cornell University, the Aviation Concentration Camp at Camp Dix in Dallas, Texas, and at Chanute Field in Rantoul, Illinois. Hill then accepted a commission as a 2nd Lieutenant in the regular Army and served as a flying instructor before receiving instruction as a bombardment pilot.

In 1919 Hill served in the Office of the Chief of the Air Corps in Washington, D.C., then in 1920 was ordered to duty with the American Army of Occupation in Germany, where he served as the Engineer Officer of the Air Service Flying Station in Weissenthurm. In 1922 he was assigned to duty with the 12th Aero Squadron stationed at Fort Bliss in El Paso, Texas, then transferred back to Chanute Field for instruction in aerial photography. After completing the course he stayed on as a student instructor.

In 1924 he returned to duty in Washington, D.C., in the Training and War Plans Division under the Chief of the Air Service. In 1925 he was ordered to duty at Mitchell Field, New York, where he was appointed Commanding Officer of the 14th Photo Section, a job he held until 1929. He then served as the Commanding Officer of the 6th Photo Section at Nichols Field in Manila. In 1932 he returned to the United States and was assigned to Wright Field in Dayton, Ohio, where he served as a test pilot and Assistant Chief of Planes and Engines in the Maintenance Unit. In 1935 he was assigned as the Chief of the Flying Branch of the Materiel Division at Wright Field, with the temporary rank of Major. His duties involved the flight test and evaluation of numerous new military aircraft designs at various contractors' plants, including the Consolidated P-30, the Martin B-10 and B-12, and many others.

On 30 October 1935 Ployer Peter Hill died as a result of injuries received from the crash of the Boeing experimental aircraft Model 299 at Wright Field. This aircraft was the prototype of what would later become the famous B-17 Flying Fortress of World War II. Major Hill was buried in Newburyport, Massachusetts, on 3 November 1935.

In 1939 the U.S. War Department named the site of the Ogden Air Depot "Hill Field" in honor of Major Ployer Peter Hill. In 1948 Hill Field was renamed Hill Air Force Base.

North American AT-6 "Texan"

No other trainer of Western origin has ever come close to the record of the T-6 for longevity and production totals. It entered service in 1936 and 21,342 were built, with many still in service today. The T-6 began life as the NA-16 prototype and first flew in April 1935. After a slow start, production accelerated rapidly just before and during WWII. This aircraft was built with a host of variants, including fixed or retractable landing gear and two different types of engines. Many of these aircraft were manufactured in Canada. After WWII they were rebuilt as the T-6G standard. There were five major variants:

- The BT-9 with the 447-KW 600 HP R-1340 engine with non-retractable landing gear
- The BT-14 with the 400 HP Pratt/Whitney R-985 engine
- The SNJ in six variants for the Navy
- The Harvard in four variants of the AT-6 for the British
- The Yale, a version of the BT-14, for Canada with 1 variant

The standard version was equipped with the R-1340 engine and had retractable landing gear. AT-6s flew here at Hill AFB during the late 1940s through the 1960s and Hill was also a storage site for the aircraft. (Display only)

Specifications:
North American AT-6 "Texan" S/N 039

Type:	North American AT-6 Texan two-seated advanced trainer
Wingspan:	42 ft
Length:	29 ft
Height:	11 ft 9 in
Weight:	3,900 empty 5,700 loaded
Engine:	1 Pratt & Whitney R-1340-49 600hp radial
Speed:	210 mph at 5,000 ft
Service ceiling:	24,200 ft
Range:	750 miles
Armament:	2 - 0.3-in (7.72mm) machine guns, 1 fixed, 1 trainable
Total produced:	10,375
Cost:	$25,672

Vultee BT-13B "Valiant"

The BT-13 was a basic trainer aircraft used for basic flight training and for blind instrument training. The rear cockpit was equipped with a curtain that could be moved forward to cover the student pilot and he would have to fly by the five basic instruments: the altimeter, airspeed indicator, compass, bank and turn indicator, and sometimes a tachometer. The BT-13 was different than the AT-6 Texan in that it did not have retractable landing gear. The first delivery to the military was in 1942, with 1,125 procured.

Specifications:

Type:	Basic Trainer
Crew:	2 (Pilot & Student)
Engine:	1 Pratt & Whitney R-985-AN-1 Wasp Jr. 450 HP
Wingspan:	42 ft 2 in
Length:	28 ft 9 in
Weight:	4,360 lbs. loaded
Height:	12 ft 5 in
Speed:	166 MPH
Ceiling:	16,500 ft
Armament:	None
Total produced:	7,832
Cost:	$23,068

Vultee BT-13B "Valiant" S/N42-90406 163

10 Apr. 1944	Delivered to the USAAF by Vultee Aircraft, Downey, CA
Apr. 1944	To Long Beach AAF, CA (Air Transport Command)
Mar. 1945	To 556th AAF Base Unit (ATC) Long Beach AAF
Apr. 1945	Disposed of as surplus
Sep. 1993	Acquired by Hill Aerospace Museum

Boeing Stearman PT-17 "Kaydet"

This is an aircraft which excites feelings about flying: open cockpit, prop-wash blasting past, fields and houses down below (but not very far), the ability to climb, turn, do acrobatics—it's all flying, and it's here in this beautifully restored biplane. Compare those feelings to being placed in a capsule (jet propelled aircraft), being pressurized, and being shot to somewhere without having really enjoyed the thrill of having controlled your flying. This was the perfect trainer for the late 1930s: a slow revving radial engine, a robust structure (it could withstand 13 Gs), highly controllable and maneuverable, and sturdy undercarriage. It began its career as the PT-13. It was well accepted and modified to the PT-17. It was used by the U.S. Navy, the USAAF, Great Britain, Venezuela, Peru, and China. At least 2,000 survived the USAAF flying training of WWII and became privately owned for spraying crops and other private activities. Many are still airworthy and are much sought after. Many are being restored. However, this aircraft is not airworthy. The wings are of wood and fabric construction the fuselage of metal tubing and fabric. HAFB had control over storage and reclamation of surplus PT-17's during the late 1940s.

Specifications:

Type:	Primary Flight Trainer
Crew:	2
Engine:	1 Continental R-670-5, 220 hp
Wingspan:	32 ft 2 in
Length:	25 ft
Height:	9 ft 2 in
Weight:	2,717 lb.
Speed:	124 mph
Range:	505 miles
Ceiling:	11,200 ft
Armament:	None
Total Produced:	10,346
Cost:	$9,896

With the ending of the war, Hill Field activities underwent a transformation. Instead of repairing and modifying the aircraft for combat, Hill Field now prepares the planes for storage. Hundreds of primary trainers are stored in one of the large repair hangars. Many top-flight army pilots started their flying careers in these very same planes.

Boeing Stearman PT-17 "Kaydet" S/N 41-25284

30 Dec. 1941	Delivered to the USAAF by Boeing Aircraft, Wichita, KS
Dec. 1941	To Maxwell AAF, AL
Jan. 1942	To 57th Elementary Flying Training (Contract) Detachment (29th Flying Training Command), Greenville Aviation School, Ocala, FL (Later, 2161st AAF Base Unit)
Aug. 1944	To 2154th AAF Base Unit (Contract Elementary Fling School, AAFFTC), Clarksdale School of Aviation, Fletcher Field, Clarksdale, MS and declared excess Nov. 1944. To Augustine Field, Madison, MS and disposed of as excess.
1980	Assigned to Hill Aerospace Museum; fully restored; hangs from the ceiling in the Gallery.

Fred Call, a museum volunteer tour guide, was a USAAF pilot in World War II. He flew many types and sizes of aircraft in his career, but says that the PT-17 was his favorite. "You could do anything with that airplane that you could do with any other airplane ever built, except fly upside down or go real fast! It was a very tough airplane, sturdy, and able to withstand high-g maneuvers and hard landings. It was light on the controls and a lot of fun to fly."

Fred explains that you couldn't fly inverted in the PT-17 because it had a gravity-fed carburetor, but you could still loop and spin, just so long as you didn't stay upside down too long. "The engine would quit if you did, but the prop was still spinning, so you could usually restart and recover anyway. It was pretty forgiving to student pilots."

One hair-raising story that Fred says took place when he was in pilot training centers around the PT-17. "An instructor pilot was up one day with a student pilot in the back seat. The IP performed a slow roll as a demonstration for the student and then called back to the guy in the back 'okay, now you try one.' There was no reaction from the back seat, so the IP called back again, this time louder, 'you try one!' Still no reaction from the back. So the IP turned and looked back to see why the student pilot was not performing the requested roll. There was no one in the back seat! The student had fallen out during the slow roll because he had forgotten to fasten his seat belt! He had on a 'chute though."

Douglas A-26C "Invader"

This light bomber was designed to fill a 1940 requirement for a single successor to the Douglas A-20 "Havoc," the Martin B-26 "Marauder," and the North American B-25 "Mitchell" light bombers. As it turned out, the aircraft was diverse in its capabilities, and it exceeded its designed specifications for speed, load, and range. All of these features led to a usefulness that extended from the end of WWII, through the Korean War, into the war in Vietnam. The first flight was made in July of 1942. It turned out it could carry twice the specified bomb load. Armament among the variant types could include a 75 mm. gun; six nose-mounted .50 cal. machine guns instead of the 75 mm. gun, and remotely controlled dorsal and ventral turrets. The A-26B was adopted as the initial production version. It included armor protection for the crew. It appeared in the European Theater of war in November 1944 with the 9th Air Force. The A-26C appeared in January 1945 with a transparent nose and was powered by two P&W R-2800 engines that produced about 2,000 hp. each. Both B and C models were used extensively in Europe. During the Korean Conflict the A-26 was the medium bomber used by the USAF. The Invader received a new lease on life in the early 1960s when a re-manufactured version, the B-26K was developed as a counter-insurgency aircraft. Each aircraft had eight .50 cal. machine guns grouped in the nose. They were used in the Vietnam war in night intruder missions. The Invader was finally phased out of service in November 1969. Hill AFB had the mission for engine repair and storage of the aircraft.

Specifications:

Type:	Light Attack Bomber
Crew:	3
Engine:	2 Pratt & Whitney R-2800, 2,000 hp each
Wingspan:	70 ft
Length:	50 ft
Height:	18 ft 6 in
Weight:	35,000 lb.
Speed:	355 mph
Cost:	$192,427
Armament:	2 tons bombs plus 10 .50 cal. machine guns
Total produced:	4,720 (for USAAF)

Douglas A-26C "Invader" SN 44-35617

15 May 1945	Delivered to USAAF by Douglas Aircraft Corporation
May 1945	To 140th Base Unit Moody Field, GA
Jan. 1946	To 4160th Base Unit, Hobbs Field, NM
Jul. 1947	To 4135th Base Unit, Hill Field, UT
Jan. 1948	Redesigned B-26C
Jan. 1951	To Ogden Air Material Area UT
Nov. 1951	To 117th Reconnaissance Technical Wing (TAC) Lawson AFB, GA
Feb. 1952	To 117th Reconnaissance Technical Wing Paris, France
Mar. 1952	Unit moved to Wiesbaden AB, Germany
Jun. 1952	Modified to RB-26C
Jul. 1952	To 10th Reconnaissance Technical Wing (USAF EUROPE) Toul-Rosiere AB, France (Periodically assigned to Furstenfieldbruck AB, Neubiberg AB, Germany, and Erding AB, Germany.
Jun. 1953	To 85th Air Defense Wing (USAFE), Erding AB, Germany
Jul. 1953	To 10th Reconnaissance Technical Wing (USAFE), Spangdahlem AB, Germany
Mar. 1954	To 737th Maintenance Group (USAFE) Chateauroux AB, France
Apr. 1954	Returned to 10th Reconnaissance Technical Wing (USAFE) Spangdahlem AB, Germany
Sep. 1955	To Manchester, England for contract Maintenance
Nov. 1955	To 184th Technical Reconnaissance Sqdn. (ANG) Ft Smith, AR
Nov. 1956	To 154th Technical Reconnaissance-Photojet Sqdn (ANG) Adams, AR
Jul. 1957	To Davis-Monthan AFB, AZ for Storage
Jan. 1958	Dropped From the USAF Inventory. Purchased by Oklahoma Aircraft Corp.
Mar. 1983	Seized by US Marshall in drug action
Mar. 1983	Flown from Maryville, CA to Travis AFB
Jan. 1984	Returned to USAF control by Court
Aug. 1990	Travis AFB, CA to Hill AFB by Truck. It is now the property of Hill Aerospace Museum.

"Project Holdoff" line at Hill

Boeing B-17G "Flying Fortress"

Best known and most revered for its ability to be severely damaged and still bring its crew home, the B-17 attracts many visitors and causes many excited and warm comments. In August 1942 B-17s of the 8th Air Force, stationed at Polebrook and Northants, England began the daylight bombing of the German war machine. According to Albert Speer, head of the German war production, those daylight raids (in which the Americans lost heavily) damaged the German war effort severely because they hit production of ball bearings, fuel, aircraft, and transportation. The B-17s, in their E, F and G variants dropped 640,000 tons of bombs compared to the 452,500 tons dropped by the more numerous B-24s. Besides service in Europe, B-17s served in the Pacific Theater, in Korea, and the Arab-Israeli war.

Our museum aircraft was manufactured by Douglas Aircraft, a subcontractor to Boeing, and was delivered to the USAAF on 1 May 1945. Since hostilities in Europe ceased on 7 May 1945 our aircraft did not see combat in WWII. The 38 bombs painted on the nose are decorations, not missions symbols. In June 1953 it was loaned to Brazil as a training aircraft. It was returned the USAF in June 1968. Transferred to the Hill Aerospace Museum in 1987, it was disassembled, and flown to Hill in a C-5, reassembled, repainted, and decorated for your enjoyment. In 1942 Hill AFB was responsible for modifications and in 1952 for major overhaul, inspection, and modification. In 1956 HAFB assumed prime depot responsibility.

Specifications:

Type:	High-altitude bomber
Crew:	6 to 10
Engines:	4 Wright Cyclone R-1820, 1,200 hp each
Wingspan:	103 ft 9 in
Length:	74 ft 4 in
Height:	15 ft 5 in
Weight:	46,650 lb.
Speed:	290 mph
Cost:	$204,370
Armament:	13 .50 cal. machine guns plus up to 8 tons of bombs
Total produced:	13,126 (all models); 2,250 G models

Boeing B-17G Flying Fortress "Short Bier" S/N 44-83663

1 May 1945	Delivered to USAAF by Douglas Aircraft Long Beach, CA
Jun. 1945	Transferred to Patterson Field, OH
Oct. 1945	Transferred to 4132nd Base Unit, (AMC) Garden City, KS
Dec. 1946	Transferred to 4141st Base Unit, (AMC) Pyote Field, TX
Apr. 1950	Transferred to 2753rd Aircraft Storage Sq. Pyote Field, TX
Mar. 1951	Transferred to Spartan Aircraft Corp. Tulsa, OK for maintenance
Jun. 1953	Turned over to the Brazilian Air Force
Jun. 1968	Returned to USAF, Wright Patterson AFB, OH
Early 1973	Loaned to Yesterday's Air Force, Chino, CA
Early 1978	Loaned to Kansas Wing, Warbird Museum, Topeka, KS
Spring 1987	Transferred to Hill Aerospace Museum From 720150 USCG Air Station, Clearwater, FL

In 1946 thousands of B-17 were sold. Prices ranged from $300 for war weary birds to $17,000 for new aircraft that cost $300,000.

Today's best estimates are that 35 of the old fortresses exist. Only about 5 or 6 are still flying. Best known are the Texas Raiders from Midland, Texas and the Sentimental Journey from Phoenix. Both are flown by Wings of the Confederate Air Force.

The Suzy-Q—First B-17 to arrive at OOAMA (19 July 1943)

During WWII, I was the Ordnance and Armament officer of the 544th Bombardment Squadron in the 384th Bombardment Group (Heavy) of the First Air Division, Eighth Air Force. We were flying B-17 Flying Fortresses out of USAAF Station 106 near the small village of Grafton Underwood, Northamptonshire, in the Midlands of England. I distinctly remember the morning of 24 July 1944. The mission that day was to drop 120 pound fragmentation bomb clusters, 42 per aircraft, to help the American and British troops break through Nazi German ground forces (in what came to be known as the "breakout at St. Lo"). I was making my final rounds of the hard stands beneath an aircraft when suddenly one cluster of six M-41 20 pound bombs fell about ten feet from the aircraft's bomb bay to the concrete hard stand below. Being so near, I was the first to see it and my first reaction was to get to those bombs fast! We were safe for the moment since none of the bombs had detonated immediately, so I yelled to get the area cleared of all the ground personnel (about 100 folks) and the six other manned and fully loaded B-17 aircraft.

I ran to where the cluster rested on the ground and began to carefully examine the bombs. I discovered that one bomb had a broken and exposed firing pin, but I was unable to remove the fuse. I yelled for my first sergeant to bring a Jeep so that we could transport the bomb to our Ordnance Shop. I picked up the bomb, cradled it in my arms and rode the short, bumpy trip to the Shop. There the bomb was quickly defused and the day's mission resumed. I'll never forget that little bit of excitement under a B-17's belly!

> —Col. Nathan H. Mazer, USAF (ret)

For his actions on 24 July 1944, Nate Mazer was awarded the Bronze Star with a "V" for valor.

B-17G DL 44-8366 "Short Bier"

Accepted by the USAAF in May of 1945 B-17G #44-83663 became one of 12,731 to be produced. First assigned to Patterson Field, Ohio in June of 1945 the airplane was to spend most of its military life in storage, either at Garden City, Kansas, or at Pyote Field, Texas. (Pyote Field was located about 25 miles east of Pecos, Texas)

In June of 1953 the aircraft was transferred to the Brazilian Air Force who flew it until 1968 when it was returned to Wright Patterson AFB. In 1973 the aircraft was loaned to Yesterdays Air Force at Chino, California. In 1978 the aircraft was flown to Topeka, Kansas, where it became part of the Kansas Warbird Museum. Its last flight under its own power came when it was transferred to a museum located on the back side of the USCG station at Clearwater, Florida. Attempts were made to keep it flying but lack of funds forced the museum to fold. The aircraft was then assigned to a museum in Cleveland, Ohio, who proved unable to raise funds and a committment of maintenence. The Hill Aerospace Museum was then selected as a final resting place.

By the time of transport even though the engines were still being "run up" the airplane had deteriotated to the point that it was un-airworthy. In the spring of 1987 a crew from Hill AFB traveled to Clearwater and dismantled the aircraft and transported it via C-5 to Hill where it was reassembled.

Since its acqustion the aircraft has been sponsored by Mr. John Lindquist who flew as the Navigator on the original Short Bier in the 493rd Bomb Squadron. The exterior restoration was completed in the spring of 1991. The aircraft is painted in the colors of the 493rd and is the third Short Bier.

The 493rd began its experience in the 8th Air Force flying B-24 aircraft but were transferred to B-17s. The nose art/nickname was transfered to the new B-17. The crew finished their tour in the B-17 which was later lost in action.

The Hill Aerospace Museum's B-17 is one of 30-35 that still exist. Less than a dozen are maintained in flying condition. B-17s were sold as salvage in 1947 at prices ranging from $300.00 to $17,000.00 depending on model and condition. B-17s dropped over 640,000 tons of bombs in WWII and just over 5,000 were lost in combat. Work continues on the interior of the aircraft with a date of completeion determined by funding and part availability.

Often times training played a significant part in the survival of bomber crews during World War II-yet it wasn't always training they had received in the military. Museum volunteer Orville Waters started out flying in B-25s and B-26s out of Marrakesh, Morocco, but following Germany's ouster from North Africa, he was transferred to Mansfield, England and the 8th Air Force. "I was a tail gunner and right-waist gunner on the Seventeens," Waters affectionately recalled of his service on B-17s. "It was late 1944, and I was on my sixteenth mission-a mission to Heidelberg, Germany-and we ran into flak that was so heavy you could walk on it!" As it turned out, the flak was too heavy and too concentrated, and as a result Water's plane, ironically named "Last Chance," sustained lethal damage. By the time the ill-fated B-17 headed out over the English Channel it was a forgone conclusion that ditching in the water would be necessary. "We ran out of fuel and ran out of altitude," laughed the personable Waters.

"We just brought her in and set her down on the water," recalled Waters on the "landing" in the English Channel. Although a daylight raid, the Channel was covered in a thick layer of fog-there was no way of telling how close to land they were, or even where land was. There were two life rafts in the B-17, each capable of holding half of the ten man crew. Waters, who made it into one of the rafts with four of his fellow crewmen, harkened back to some training that he'd had before joining the military: "I was very involved with the Scout program, and I never loose direction." Waters heard what sounded like breakers hitting on a shore, and as a result his raft headed in that direction. About an hour and a half later, his life raft landed on the English Coast. Sadly, the other raft and its five crewmen were never seen again. Orville Waters is still actively involved with the Boy Scouts of America.

"Short Bier" coming out of a C-5 at Hill

Consolidated B-24D "Liberator"

Long-range USAAF bomber. The XB-24 prototype (Model 32) flew in December 1939. It used many features pioneered in the preceding Model 31 flying boat, including the high aspect "Davis" wing. Beginning in 1940 production from four companies produced a total of 18,482 aircraft. The Liberator possessed good handling characteristics, considerable structural strength, and enormous versatility as a bomber, maritime reconnaissance, and transport aircraft. It was used extensively as a bomber in the Pacific, Mediterranean, and European theaters. The Liberator's most famous single exploit was the low level daylight raid on the Romanian oil fields at Ploesti. One of the most famous of these B-24s was the "Utah Man" that was flown by Col. Walter Stewart from Benjamin, Utah. Principal users were Australia, Canada, Great Britain, and the US.

Specifications:

Type:	Heavy Bomber
Crew:	8-12
Engines:	4 1,200 hp Pratt & Whitney R-1830-65 radial
Wingspan:	110 ft
Length:	67 ft 2 in
Height:	18 ft
Weight:	36,500 lb. empty
Speed:	290 mph at 25,000 feet
Service ceiling:	28,000 ft
Range:	2,100 miles
Cost:	$289,276
Armament:	10 .50 cal. machine guns in nose, dorsal, ventral and tail. Up to 12,800 lb. of bombs in the two beam positions.

Consolidated B-24D "Liberator" S/N 41-23908

Date of Manufacture: 24 Sep. 1942

18 Jan. 1943   Pilot Ernie Pruett and his eight-man crew plus five other B-24s took off from the air base on Adak Island for a bombing mission over Kiska Island, which was held by the Japanese. Shortly after take off two planes returned to base with engine trouble. Unfortunately by then the field as totally socked in by the fog. One of the two planes crashed into some parked aircraft while trying to land. Four of the planes continued on the mission, but due to bad weather they never found the target.

Pruett knew that he didn't have enough fuel to return to Adak Island so he began to look for a place to set his B-24 and crew down as safely as possible. When he saw a small brown spot of alluvial plain he headed for it. By this time the fuel gages were registering empty. Pruett belly flopped into that small brown spot and skidded about a 1000 ft. before the plane came to rest. Fortunately only one crew member was injured.

They had landed on Great Sitkin Island about twenty miles northeast of Adak. The Navy picked them up by ship later that day.

That was the last Ernie Pruett of Carlsbad, California knew of his aircraft for 52 years. At the age of 80 he returned to assist in the recovery of his aircraft for the Hill Aerospace Museum. It was recovered in August 1995 by The Air Force Foundation of Utah. Twenty members from Hill AFB worked 10 to 18 hours a day to recover it. The B-24 is now awaiting restoration. A contract for restoration was let in July 1996 with restoration in progress. It will take 15 months from time of contract to go ahead, at a cost of approximately $400,000.

Source M/Gen. Rex Hadley AFHFOU.

The "belly flopped" B-24 as it looked at recovery (1995)

North American B-25 "Mitchell"

In the late 1930s the US Army Air Corps needed a new attack bomber. Built as a private venture, the NA-40-1 prototype flew in January 1939. The design was improved as the NA-62, and in September 1939 the USAAC placed its first order. The first 184 B-25 Mitchells entered service in 1941. The USA's entry into the Second World War saw a rapid growth in production as 9,816 aircraft were produced. The Mitchell remained essentially unaltered in airframe and power plant. It was revised with heavier and more varied offensive payload, improved defensive firepower, protective armor, and more fuel in self-sealing tanks. The most important models that were built 1,916 B-25C, 1,000 B-25H, and 4,318 of the B-25Js. The G and H models were special attack and anti-ship types with a 75-mm (2.95 inch) gun in the nose. The Mitchells were used in all the theaters of operations. The B-25B had dorsal and ventral turrets. The B-25C and D had ventral bomb racks, the G, J, and D's had a glazed nose and later a solid nose with eight guns. The Mitchell was used for the one-way "Doolittle Raid" on Japan, which was launched from the aircraft carrier Hornet on 18 April 1942.

Specifications:

Type:	Medium Bomber
Crew:	5
Engines:	2 1,700-hp Wright R-2600-13 radial
Wing Span:	67 ft 7 in
Length:	51 ft
Height:	15 ft 7 in
Weight:	Empty 19,975 lb. Gross 36,047 lb.
Speed:	275 at 13,000 ft.
Service ceiling:	23,800 ft
Range:	2,700 miles
Armament:	18 .50 Cal. machine guns + 3,200 lb. bombs or one 2,000 lb. torpedo.
Cost:	$142,194
Total Produced:	11,000

North American B-25 "Mitchell" S/N 44-86772

28 Jun. 1945:	Accepted by USAAF
29 Jun. 1945	To Sacramento CA for storage
25 Jul. 1945	To Salinas, CA For Storage
4 Sep. 1945	To Independence, MO., for storage, 4185 Base Storage Unit
3 Aug. 1947	To Pykote AAF, TX Base Unit Storage
19 Oct. 1949	To Pykote AAF, TX 2753rd Air Storage Sq. Maintenance
27 Oct. 1949	Brookley Field, AL for Maintenance
27 Jan. 1950	To 1050 Maintenance Service Unit Andrews AFB, MD
22 Aug. 1952	To 1401 Air Base Wing-Utility, Andrews AFB, MD
Oct. 1954	To Birmingham, AL for Hayes conversion
Jan. 1955	To 1401 Air Base Wing, Andrews AFB, MD
Dec. 1957	To 1001 Air Base Wing, Andrews AFB, MD
Nov. 1958	To Davis-Monthan AFB, AZ for storage
Jan. 1959	Davis-Monthan AFB, Declared Surplus
Jul. 1959	Sold By USAF to National Metals, Phoenix, AZ
Nov. 1960	Sold to Frank Froehling, Coral Gables, FL for $3000
Dec. 1960	FAA inspection reveals 5,695 hours on airframe Oct. 1961 Sold to Davis-Brown, Hialeah, FL and modified for cargo work
Nov. 1964	Letter from Mr. Brown to FAA requesting registration be canceled as he had lost physical control of the aircraft in January 1962 in Argentina.
Dec. 1964	Registration Canceled
Note:	Our B-25 was found in a farmer's field in Argentina in 1962 after it had made a forced landing due to a fuel or engine problem. It was smuggling cigarettes into Argentina from Paraguay at the time of the incident. During the landing in a rough field, the nose wheel collapsed and the nose was damaged. It was donated to a local flying club, who moved it to their airfield where it sat on display for over 27 years.
	In 1990 it was returned from Argentina by Don Wittingham of Ft. Lauderdale, Florida where it sat in pieces at his hanger until it was rebuilt for the Hill Aerospace Museum.

Boeing B-29 "Superfortress"

The B-29 replaced the B-17 and the B-24. It was so well designed that production modifications were minimal. When one was forced down in Russia, the Soviets copied it and in 1947 displayed it to the world as the TU-4. Because of its great range and large bomb load, hundreds of them flew the great ocean expanse from the Mariannas Islands in 1944 and 1945 to bomb Japan. (The B-29 was never used in the European theater). On 6 August 1945, a B-29 like this one dropped the atomic bomb on Hiroshima, and three days later a second bomb was dropped on Nagasaki. Three days later, Japan indicated willingness to surrender. General Doolittle said the B-29 made it unnecessary to invade Japan. A book by Joseph Marx, *Seven Hours to Zero*, should be a must for readers wanting to understand the experience of the crew of the "Enola Gay" over Hiroshima. Our aircraft was manufactured and delivered to the USAAF in August 1945. Our aircraft was assigned to Tooele Army Depot for nerve gas testing in November 1953. It withstood the indignations of testing, ravages of weather, vandals, and those who took the instruments until 1979. It was acquired by the Museum, and brought to HAFB, where it was reassembled by the 2952nd RAM team and volunteers working under Mel Blanscett seven days a week for eight months. Very few still exist. HAFB was a spares control depot which served all B-29 stations in 1945. A total of 3965 were produced and all were phased out in 1957, the year modified B-29s were placed in storage at HAFB.

Specifications:

Type:	High-altitude bomber, recon
Crew:	9-11
Engines:	4 Wright R-3350, 2,200hp ea.
Speed:	357 mph
Range:	4,100 miles
Ceiling:	31,850 ft
Wingspan:	141 ft 3 in
Length:	99 ft
Height:	29 ft 7 in
Weight:	133,500 lb.
Armament:	12 .50 cal. machine guns + 20mm cannon (tail); 20,000 lb. bombs
Total produced:	4,221
Cost:	$605,360

Boeing B-29 "Superfortress" S/N 44-86408

Aug. 6 1945	Delivered to the USAAF by Glen L. Martin Co., Omaha, NB
Aug. 1945	To 4141st Base Unit, Pyote Field, TX
May 1946	To 4121st Base Unit, Kelly Field, TX
Jun. 1948	To 97th Bomb Group (SAC) Biggs AFB, TX
Jun. 1949	To 4002nd base Services Sqdn. (SAC) Campbell Field, KY
Oct. 1949	To 43rd Bomb Group (SAC) Davis-Monthan AFB, AZ
Aug. 1950	To 9th Bomb Wing (SAC) Fairfield, CA
Feb. 1953	To 9th Bomb Wing (SAC) Travis AFB, CA
May 1953	To Wright Development Center, Wright-Patterson AFB, OH June 1953 To 6750th Chemical and Ordnance Test (Air Research and Development Command) Hill AFB, UT
Nov. 1953	Dropped from USAF inventory at Dugway Proving Grounds, UT
Fall 1983	To Hill for restoration and Museum display

One of the Museum volunteers (who wishes to remain anonymous) was a B-29 pilot during World War II, flying out of India. He says the B-29 was a dream to fly, handling "like a Cadillac" on the controls, but was plagued by lots of engine problems. "The engines were poor, underpowered, and overheated a lot. We received the first B-29s ever built and the engines even had to be changed out on them *before* our first combat mission was flown! It was so hot in India we were always having engine overheating problems. It was nothing for the temperature at the airfield to hit 120 degrees, with very high humidity. It was miserable! I witnessed a B-29 takeoff one day when the spark plugs blew right out of one of the engines it was so hot! I was glad it wasn't me."

He says that the aircraft mechanics tried everything to fix the B-29's engine problems and reduce the chronic overheating. "We even took tin snips and cut the cowl flaps off right down to the actuator arms, to let the cooling air in the engines without having to leave the cowl flaps open on takeoff. If you left them open on takeoff in that heat and humidity, the engines weren't strong enough to keep the open flaps from stalling out the wings! So we cut them off to get the cooling air without affecting the slipstream and the lift of the wings. But despite the engine problems the B-29 was a real honey to fly."

Haggerty's Hag is disassembled at Dugway Proving Ground before transport to Hill AFB.
US Army photo

De Havilland C-7A "Caribou"

The C-7 prototype flew on 30 July 1958 and was called the Buffalo by the Canadian Manufacturer. The U.S. Army ordered five evaluation aircraft and they were designated the YAC-rs. The first of these were delivered in October 1959 and satisfactory results of the trials resulted in an additional order of seven. The additional aircraft were delivered in January 1961. It was then designated the C-7 Caribou. In May 1961 an additional fifteen were ordered. The C-7 Caribou can carry twenty-four fully-equipped troops, three tons of freight or fourteen casualty litters. The C-7 was used extensively in Vietnam by the US Army and USAF. The Museum aircraft came from the U.S. Army Reserve in Salt Lake City, Utah. Hill AFB had the repair and the storage responsibility for the P&W R-2000 engines used on C-7 aircraft.

Specifications:

Type:	Utility Transport, 30-40 Passengers
Crew:	3
Power Plant:	2 Pratt & Whitney R-2000-13
Wingspan:	96 ft 1/2 in
Length:	72 ft 7 in
Height:	31 ft 9 in
Weight:	Empty 16,850 lb., loaded: 49,200 lb.
Ceiling:	31,000 ft
Speed:	182 mph (cruising) 290 mph
Range:	691 miles
Cost	N/A

De Havilland C-7A "Caribou" S/N 63-9757
(Or De Havilland DHC-5 Buffalo)

Manufacturer:	De Havilland Canada, Toronto, Ontario, Canada, As CV-2A For the US Army.
31 Dec. 1966	Transferred to USAF from the 17th Aviation Company, Phu Cat AB, Vietnam Jan. 1967 To 483rd Troop Carrier (Medium) Wing PAF Phu Cat AB
Jan. 1968	Unit became the 483rd Tactical Airlift Wing (Deployments to Cam Ranh Bay AB, Vietnam and Kadena AB, Japan)
Sep. 1971	To Sacramento Air Material Area, McClellan AFB, CA
Dec. 1971	To Warner Robbins Air Material, Maxwell AFB, AL
May 1972	To 908th Tactical Airlift Group (USAF Reserve) Maxwell AFB, AL
Sep. 1977	To 357 Tactical Airlift Sq. (AFRES) Maxwell AFB, AL
Oct. 1983	Dropped from inventory by transfer to US Army
Aug. 1991	On the 23 of August flown to Hill AFB for display at the Aerospace Museum from 211th AVN Gp. USAR SLC, UT

Beechcraft C-45H "Expeditor"

The C-45 was the WWII military version of the popular Beechcraft Model 18 commercial light transport. Beech built a total of 4,526 of these aircraft for the Army Air Forces between 1939 and 1945 in four versions, the AT-7 "Navigator" navigation trainer, the AT-11 "Kansas" bombing-gunnery trainer, the C-45 "Expeditor" utility transport, and the F-2 for aerial photography and mapping. The AT-7 and AT-11 versions were well known to WWII navigators and bombardiers for most of these men received their training in these aircraft. Thousands of AAF pilot cadets also were given advanced training in twin-engines Beech airplanes. During the early 1950s, Beech completely rebuilt 900 C-45s for the Air Force. They received new serial numbers and were designated C-45Gs and C-45Hs. They remained in service until 1963 for administrative and light cargo duties. HAFB was responsible for C-45 maintenance from 1947-50, and for storage in 1953. Many still remain popular with private and commercial owners.

Specifications:

Type:	Light transport and trainer, Passengers 6-8
Crew:	2
Engines:	2 P&W R-985 Wasp Jr., 450 hp each
Wingspan:	47 ft 8 in
Length:	34 ft 3 in
Height:	9 ft 2 in
Weight:	9,300 lb.
Speed:	225 mph
Range:	7,000 miles
Ceiling:	20,000 ft
Armament:	None
Total produced:	1,401
Cost:	$52,507

Beechcraft C-45H "Expeditor" S/N 52-10862

27 Aug. 1945	Delivered to USAAF by Beech Aircraft Corp. Wichita, KS
Aug. 1954	To 141st Fighter-Bomber Sq. (Air National Guard) McGuire AFB, NJ
Oct. 1954	To 119th Fighter-Bomber (ANG) Newark Airport, NJ
Feb. 1956	To 150th Aeromedical Transport Sq.(ANG)Light, Newark, NJ
Sep. 1958	To 141st Fighter-Interceptor Sq. (ANG) McQuire AFB, NJ
Nov. 1960	To 141st Tactical Fighter Sq. (ANG) McQuire AFB, NJ June 1960 To 2704th Aircraft Storage and Disposition Group, (AMC) Davis-Monthan AFB, AZ
Feb. 1963	Dropped from USAF inventory
Oct. 1985	Aircraft ferried from Moore AFB, Mission Hill, TX to Hill AFB, By the Department of Agriculture.

The C-45 H in flight

Douglas C-47 "Gooney Bird"

Eisenhower said it was one of four tools that brought us victory in WWII. Affectionately called "Gooney Bird" and "Biscuit Bomber," graceful, proud, extremely capable, it has filled every role of transport: recon (it night-photographed a key French city with Harold Edgerton's new, huge strobe light on June 5-6, 1944 to show the Allies that German troops were not there); paratroop drops (821 C-47's helped the 82nd and 101st Airborne Divisions in their assault roles in WWII); towed gliders; casualty evacuation; Berlin Airlift; the HC-47A did search and rescue work; dropped flares; attacked ground troops in Vietnam as "Puff the Magic Dragon"; and having served the war roles so well, many returned to civilian life after WWII as commercial transports. Over 1,000 are still flying around the world, two of them from Ogden, Utah's Hinkley Airport for the U.S. Forest Service. One DC-3, flying for an airline out of Boston, has over 90,000 hours flight time. The C-47 (DC-3)has flown for nearly every flag in the world, and has also flown on skis and floats. Because of its sturdy construction, not one has ever crashed because of structural failure; maybe because of pilot error, lack of fuel, extreme weather conditions, or enemy action, but never because of structural failure. It has been called one of the most important airplanes in aviation history and one of the most beloved airplanes ever built. The story of this type of aircraft began in 1932 as the commercial airliner DC-3. Because of WWII the military took all DC-3s into military service. Thousands more were manufactured as C-47s with wide cargo doors. Hill AFB had three C-47 assigned until the end of 1960. Our aircraft was manufactured in November 1944 and came to the HAFBM in 1983.

Specifications:

Type:	Transport for troops, personnel, cargo
Crew:	2-3
Wingspan:	95 ft
Length:	63 ft 9 in
Height:	17 ft
Weight:	26,000 lb.
Engines:	2 P&W R-1830, 1,200 hp. each
Speed:	Cruising 185 mph; Max. 229 mph
Cost:	$138,000
Armament:	As "Puff the Magic Dragon:" 3 7.62mm mini-guns (6,000 rpm)

Douglas C-47D "Gooney Bird" 43-49281

Manufacturer:	Douglas Aircraft Corp, Oklahoma City, OK
Nov. 1944	Delivered to USAAF
Nov. 1944	To 2527th Base Unit, South Plains Field, TX
Nov. 1945	To 2517th Base Unit, Ellington Field, TX
Mar. 1945	To 3000th Base Unit, Orange County Field, CA
May 1945	To 3008th Base Unit, Minter Field, CA
Jun. 1945	Returned to 3000th, Orange County Field, CA
Oct. 1945	To 35th Base Unit, Bolling Field, DC
Mar. 1946	To Brooks Field, TX
Jun. 1946	Returned to Bolling, DC
Jun. 1947	Modified to the C-47D
Mar. 1948	To 4112th Base Unit, Olmsted AFB, PA
May 1948	To 16th Special Air Missions Bolling AFB, DC
Jul. 1948	To 1100th Special Missions Group, Bolling AFB, DC Modified to VC-C-47D
Dec. 1949	To 1114th Special Air Missions Sq., O'Hara Airport, Chicago, IL
Dec. 1949	To 3345th Tech. Training Wing (ATC) Chanute AFB, IL
Mar. 1950	Returned to 1114th at O'Hara
Jan. 1951	To 90th Air Base Group (SAC) Forbes AFB, KS
Mar. 1951	Returned to 1114th at O'Hara
Jun. 1951	To Middletown Air Material Area
Oct. 1951	To Wright Development Center, Wright-Patterson AFB, OH
Nov. 1951	To 1110th Special Missions Group, Bolling, DC
Jun. 1953	To 1299th Transport Sq. (MATS), Bolling AFB, DC
Oct. 1954	To Hollman Air Development Center, Hollman AFB, NM
Nov. 1959	To Cambridge Research Center, Lawrence G. Hanscom Field, MA
Jul. 1962	To 3245th Air Base Wing Lawrence G. Hanscom Field, MA
Sep. 1962	Dropped From USAF inventory and turned over to the US Army
Feb. 1975	Departed Davis-Monthan AFB, AZ for Ogden, UT, to the Forest Service. It was used primarily for Smoke Jumpers and Para-cargo. Summer Stations were Boise and Ogden.
Sep. 1983	Departed Ogden City Airport for HAFB on the 23rd of September for the Aerospace Museum.

Total 16,082 Flight hours

Douglas C-54 "Skymaster"

At the outbreak of WWII there were no four-engined transports immediately available for service use. In early 1942 the USAAF took over the DC-4 production line, changing the designation to C-54. Sixty-one of these large four-engined aircraft had been ordered before the prototype flew. Delivery of the first aircraft was in 1942. The DC-4E had first flown on 7 June 1938. Air Transport Command used 1,163 throughout WWII. Their contributions to victory were immeasurable. In their total of 79,642 flights across various oceans only three losses occurred. An outstanding safety record. A record which seems nearly impossible even today. They were widely used in the Korean War, operating the Pacific Airlift. Hill AFB had two C-54s assigned until the late 1960s. Our aircraft was manufactured by Douglas Aircraft at Santa Monica, California and delivered to the USAAF 26 June 1945. It was acquired by the Museum in February 1992.

Specifications:

Type:	Troop and cargo transport
Crew:	5 With accommodation for 42 troops
Speed:	Cruising 227 mph
Ceiling:	22,300 ft
Height:	27 ft 6 in
Weight:	62,000 lb. gross
Wing Span:	117 ft 6 in
Length:	93 ft 11 in
Power Plant:	4 P&W R-2000, 1,450 hp
Armament:	None
Cost:	$1,180,000

Douglas C-54G-1 "Skymaster" S/N 45-502

26 Jun. 1945	Delivered to the USAAF by Douglas Aircraft, Santa Monica, CA
Jun. 1945	To Memphis, TN
Jul. 1945	To Karachi, India (10th AF), Morrison AAF, FL
Oct. 1945	To 4136th AAF Base Unit ATSC Tinker AAF, OK
Apr. 1946	To 4119th AAF Base AMC, Brookley AAF, AL
Jun. 1946	To 1103rd AAF Base Unit AMC, Morrison AAF, FL
May 1947	To 1377th AF Base Unit ATC, Westover AAF, MA
May 1948	To Germany participation in the Berlin Airlift
Aug. 1949	To 1700th Air Transport Group MATS, Kelly AFB, TX
Sep. 1949	To 1271st Air Transport Sq. MATS, Great Falls AFB, MT
Oct. 1951	To 1708th Ferrying Gp MATS, Kelly AFB, TX
Mar. 1952	To 1273rd Air Transport Sq. MATS, Haneda AB, Japan
Jun. 1952	To 99th Air Transport Sq. MATS, Haneda AB, Japan
Oct. 1952	To 47th Air Transport Sq. MATS, Hickham AFB, HI
Jan. 1953	To 83rd Air Transport Sq. MATS, Grenier AFB, NH
Feb. 1953	To 35th Air Transport Sq. MATS, Kindley AFB, Bermuda Deployed to Ernst Harmon AFB, Newfoundland
Aug. 1955	To 17th Air Transport Sq. MATS, Charleston AFB, SC Deployed to Thule AFB, Greenland, Goose Bay AB And Sondrestromfjord Af, Greenland
Oct. 1956	To 1608th Maintenance Group, MATS, Charleston AFB, SC
Feb. 1957	To 1608th Field Maint. Sq. MATS, Charleston AFB, SC Deployed to RAF Burtonwood, UK
Feb. 1958	To 3499th Field Training Wing ATC, Chanute AFB, IL
Jun. 1959	To Sheppard Tech Training Center ATC, Sheppard AFB, TX
Jul. 1962	To 3750th Maintenance Sp. Gp ATC, Sheppard AFB, TX Deployed to Eglin AFB, FL
Oct. 1968	To Air Proving Ground Center, AFSC, Eglin AFB, FL
Dec. 1968	To Air Armament Test Center, AFSC, Eglin AFB, FL
Nov. 1969	To 3750th Maintenance Support Gp ATC, Sheppard AFB, TX
Mar. 1973	To Military Aircraft Storage and Disposition Center, Davis-Monthan AFB, AZ
Nov. 1974	Dropped from inventory as surplus and sold to Haiti Air Freight Intl., Miami, FL
Feb. 1992	Delivered to Hill AFB, UT for Hill Aerospace Museum

An often overlooked facet of aviation history during World War II is the countless number of female pilots who served their country. One such pilot is museum volunteer Mary Worrell who enlisted in the U.S. Navy in 1943. "In that first year, the Navy sent out fliers looking for people that were interested in flight training," reminisced Worrell. Following a positive response to this appeal of the Navy, she began her training at the Naval Flight Training Test Center in Maryland. After almost a year of training she emerged as a Transport Airmen on the R5D (C-54 classification for the USAF and DC-4 classification for commercial) in the Naval Air Transport Service. "The Navy considered us Transport Airmen, but we had co-pilot duties," recalled Worrell.

Flying the R5D for the Naval Air Transport Service between 1944 and 1946 provided her with a diverse collection of experiences. "I've flown in hurricanes, with engines on fire, and after the war I even flew with white mice," remembered Worrell. The mice, generally not considered to be your standard VIP Navy passenger, were destined for the atomic tests in the Bikini Atoll. "They stink like the devil," smiled Worrell. Among the various memories of this soft-spoken former Navy pilot is one in particular that brings home the tragedy of war. "Towards the end of World War II we were bringing home class one psychotics-they were shell shocked," reflected Worrell. These unfortunate servicemen were being flown back from Europe to Bethesda Naval Hospital in Maryland for treatment. Worrell's section of the flight covered Guantánamo Bay to the United States; along with her were the pilot, a nurse, and a corpsman. "We had the patients in straight jackets, and since it was a long flight, we would let them out one at a time to exercise and eat," explained Worrell. "Upon being let out, one of them went right for the door of the R5D and began to open it." It took the strength of everybody involved to pull him away from the door and restrain him. When the patient was once again safely secured, he was asked why he had tried to leave the airplane? He replied, "I was just going out to get my mail."

Fairchild C-119G "Flying Boxcar"

The first C-119 was delivered in 1947. It was strong, reliable, and versatile, serving all of the branches of the United States military and many foreign countries including Canada, Belgium, Brazil, Ethiopia, India, Italy, Taiwan, and Vietnam. Its pod-shaped fuselage, with clam-shell doors that open fully, allow straight-in loading to a floor that is the same height as a truck bed and the entire inside is accessible. Its volume is 93% of a railroad box car, thus the nickname. The high-mounted twin tail booms allowed a truck to access the fuselage for on and off loading of cargo with no obstructions. Forty-two paratroopers could jump clear of the fuselage with no fear of hitting the tail surfaces. It could transport and drop heavy military equipment and was frequently used for casualty evacuation. It made the first mid-air recovery of the space capsule Discoverer XIV, snagging its chute at 8,000 feet over the Pacific ocean 400 miles from Hawaii. The most produced model, the G, was modified into a gunship for ground attack to harass enemy troops and suppress anti-aircraft fire. The weapons were 4 x 7.62mm miniguns or 2 x 20mm cannon guided by a target illuminator. Our G model aircraft was built in October 1953 but did not receive the gun packs or auxiliary jets as some G models did. Production of the C-119 ended in 1955. This aircraft came to Hill AFB for the Museum in 1985.

Specifications:

Type:	Tactical transport and gunship
Crew:	4-5
Engines:	2 Pratt & Whitney R-4360-20, 3,500 hp each
Cruise:	200 mph
Wingspan:	109 ft 3 in
Length:	86 ft 6 in
Weight:	74,000 lb.
Height:	26 ft 4 in
Armament:	Pods for 4 7.62mm miniguns or 2 M61 20mm cannon
Cost:	$480,000

Fairchild C-119G "Flying Boxcar" S/N 22107

Oct. 1952:	Delivered to USAF by Fairchild
Oct. 25 1952	To 25th AMB
Nov. 1953	To 1003 TSD Vulcan Det.
Dec. 1954	To NWI Edmonton
Nov. 1956	To CPARC Ltd. Vulcan Alta
Jul. 1957	To NWI Edmonton
Nov. 1957	To 1002 TSD NWI Q.C.RCAF 458
Jun. 1958	To 436 T. Sq.
Jun. 1961	To WATC
Nov. 1961	To 1002 TSD Edmonton
Nov. 1962	To 435 NAMD
Dec. 1962	To 1002 TSD Edmonton
Jul. 1964	To AR1005 TSD Saskatoon
Aug. 1965	To APDAL Bristol Areo Industries Limited, 1005
	TSD Bristol Saskatoon
	From December 1954 to July 1964, aircraft was flown by the Royal Canadian Air Force.
22 Aug. 1967	Sold to Frank Shelly of Los Angeles. It was then sold to Hawkins and Powers of Greybull, Wyoming (fire fighters).
5 Nov. 1985	It was flown to Hill Air Force Base from Greybull, Wyoming.

The C-119 State of Utah

The 733rd Troop Carrier Squadron was an Air Force Reserve transport service stationed at Hill AFB for several years. Early in 1958 the unit began receiving C-119 aircraft to replace their aging C-46 cargo planes.

In the winter of 1958 hundreds of members of the U.S. Army's 82nd Airborne came to Hill AFB for a practice airdrop with the 733rd TCS. They spent one night on the field west of Base Ops in their pup tents and the next day loaded into all 18 of the 733rd's C-119s, twelve to fifteen paratroopers per plane. The flight of aircraft took off and headed through Ogden Canyon at low-level — "low enough to look straight out the windows and see the canyon walls out to the sides of the aircraft" one aircrew member recalls. After winding through the narrow canyon they headed across Ogden Valley and turned up the South Fork of the Ogden River toward Monte Cristo. Climbing through the canyons toward the pass, the C-119s turned north across Ant Flats, the designated drop zone. Flying in formation up the valley, the 82nd Airborne performed a flawless mass jump on their target.

As was their custom, the men of the Airborne psyched themselves up just before the jump by stamping their boots in unison on the floor of the aircraft while still seated along the sides. Then they stood and turned toward the rear jumpdoors of the C-119, hooking their jump harnesses to the overhead static lines. Each man checked the gear and hook-up of the man in front of him and when the signal light came on they all moved toward the open doors.

On each of the C-119s an Air Force Reserve aircrew member stood in the doorway as the "Jump Master," watching closely as the men of the Airborne filed past to make the jump. On one particular C-119, as the Airborne soldiers were hurrying out of the plane, the last man in line grabbed the Jump Master (who was required to wear a parachute in order to work near the open jump doors) and held onto him as he leaped from the plane!

The jumpers all landed in the target zone in armpit-deep snow, including the startled Air Force Jump Master. After struggling to free themselves from the snow and their parachutes, all of the jumpers marched to waiting Army trucks and rode the long trip back to Hill Field. The Jump Master, tired and cold from his impromptu indoctrination into the 82nd Airborne, was joyously reunited with the rest of his waiting aircrew later that night.

Fairchild-Chase C-123 "Provider"

The C-123, designed by Chase Aircraft, began its career in 1949 as a heavy assault glider. Engines were added later. When Chase could not deliver the requested aircraft, the USAF awarded the contract to Fairchild in 1954. It featured high-mounted wings and tail surfaces on a pod-type fuselage which made for unobstructed easy rear end on and off loading. Because of its powerful engines, it had excellent short field take off and landing capability. It could carry sixty-one fully equipped troops or evacuate fifty patients on litters plus six attendants. Several were converted to AC-123K gunships with 7.62mm miniguns for counter-insurgency operations. In 1966, some models, including this aircraft, were fitted with two 2,850 lb. thrust GE J-85 turbojet engines mounted on pylons outboard of each engine. These were for emergency use. There were many other users of the C-123 aircraft besides the USAF and the U.S. Coast Guard, which include Cambodia, Saudi Arabia, South Korea, Thailand, and Venezuela. Our aircraft was operated by the Alaska Air National Guard until 1976. We've been asked if it lands on water. No, it does not land on the water in spite of the boxy appearance of its fuselage. It was an excellent support and general utility aircraft. The two tubes on the nose are pilot tubes, part of the pilot's altitude and airspeed indicators. Ogden Air Logistics Center had prime supply, maintenance, and specialized depot responsibilities for this aircraft beginning in 1972. The UC-123B model was used for spraying defoliants in Vietnam. Production stopped in September 1969. This aircraft was used at Hill AFB for mosquito abatement and on the desert for spraying grasshoppers.

Specifications:

Type:	Tactical support transport and gunship
Crew:	2-4
Engines:	2 P&W R-2800, 2,500 hp ea. W/ 2 GE-85 aux. turbojets of 2,850 thrust each
Wingspan:	110 ft
Length:	76 ft 3 in
Height:	34 ft 1 in
Weight:	71,000 lb.
Speed:	245 mph
Armament:	7.62 miniguns
Cost:	N/A

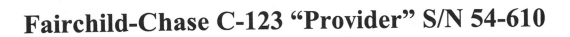

Fairchild-Chase C-123 "Provider" S/N 54-610

10 Dec. 1955	Delivered to the USAF by Fairchild Corporation
Dec. 1955	To 309th Troop Carrier Group, Assault, Fixed Wing (TAC) Ardmore AFB, OK
May 1956	To 60th Troop Carrier Wing, Medium USAF, Dreux AB, France
Jun. 1958	To 2584th Air Reserve Flying Center AFRES, Memphis, TN
Nov. 1959	To Middletown AMA, PA for work
Dec. 1959	To 445th Trop Carrier Wing, Assault AFRes, Memphis, TN
Feb. 1963	To 920th Material Sq. AFRes, Memphis, TN
Mar. 1963	To 445th Troop Carrier Wing AFRes, Memphis, TN
Jun. 1963	To 920th Troop Carrier Gp. Assault AFRes, Memphis, TN
Oct. 1965	To 401st Tactical Fighter Wing TAC, England AFB, LA
Dec. 1965	To 1st Air Commando Wing, TAC, England AFB, LA
Apr. 1966	To Fairchild, Hagerstown, MD, for work
Feb. 1967	To 4410th Combat Crew Training Wg. TAC, England AFB, LA
Jul. 1969	To 1st Special Operations Gp TAC, Eglin AFB, FL
Sep. 1969	To 317th Tact Airlift Wing TAC, Lockbourne AFB, OH
Aug. 1971	To 4410th Special Operations Training Gp TAC, England AFB, LA
Apr. 1972	To 911th Airlift Gp AFRes, Greater Pittsburgh Airport, Pittsburgh, PA
Jun. 1980	To 731st Tact Airlift Sq. AFRes, Westover AFB, MA
Aug. 1982	To Davis-Monthan AFB, AZ for storage Aircraft turned over to US Forest Service
	This Aircraft was used in the movie "Tucker" and the James Bond movie "The Living Daylights" and in at least two TV shows.
May 1989	To Hill AFB Museum from US Forest Service

Douglas C-124 "Globemaster II"

Many USAF transport aircraft were used during the 11 months of the Berlin airlift but only one, the Fairchild C-82, was designed especially as a military transport. This experience indicated the need for a new heavy transport aircraft. Among the first to be built was the C-124, based on the C-74 Globemaster design. One C-74 aircraft had taken part in the Berlin Airlift. C-124 development began in 1947 using the same wing, power plant, and tail unit as the C-74, but with a deep fuselage with clam shell nose loading doors and a built-in ramp. It retained the elevator hoist amidships which had been a feature of the C-74. The Globemaster II has a larger, but lighter fuselage. The 28th Logistic Support Group used the C-124 at Hill AFB starting on 8 July 1953. The last C-124 assigned to the 945th Military Airlift Group (Reserve) flew out of Hill AFB on 27 November 1972.

Specifications:

Type:	Heavy cargo transport capable of handling 68,500 lb. of cargo, 200 passengers or 127 stretchers
Crew:	8
Power Plant:	4 R-4360, 3,800 hp
Wing Span:	174 ft 2 in
Length:	130 ft
Height:	48 ft 4 in
Weight:	216,000 lb. gross
Speed:	271 mph max.; cruising: 230 mph
Armament:	None
Cost:	$1,646,000

Douglas C-124 "Globemaster II" S/N 53-0050

4 May 1955	Delivered to USAF by Douglas Aircraft Corp. Long Beach, CA
May 1955	To 15th Air Transport Sq. (Heavy) MATS Dover, DE
Oct. 1955	To 6606th Air Base Wing Northeast Air Command, Goose Bay, Labrador
Oct. 1955	To 15th Air Transport Sq. Heavy, NEAC, Dover AFB, DE
Nov. 1956	To 1607th Flightline Main. Sq. MATS, Dover AFB, DE
Feb. 1958	To 1607th Air Transport Wing Heavy, MATS, Dover AFB, DE
Jun. 1965	To 1501st Air Transport Wing Heavy, MATS, Hill AFB, UT
Aug. 1965	To 62nd Air Transport Wing Heavy, MATS, McChord AFB, WA
Nov. 1969	To 151st Military Airlift Gp, Air National Guard, Salt Lake City, UT
Jun. 1972	Dropped from the USAF inventory by transfer to US Army
Oct. 1992	To Hill AFB Aerospace Museum from Aberdeen Proving Grounds, MD

The 28th Logistics Support Squadron was assigned to the Ogden Air Materiel Area at Hill AFB beginning in July of 1953. The primary mission of the squadron's huge C-124C aircraft was to provide air transportation in direct worldwide support of special weapons activities.

During the period of time that the 28th was assigned to the Logistics Support function, most of our missions were classified. In order to maintain security, each aircraft was assigned a maintenance crew consisting of one flight mechanic and four hazard pay mechanics to perform all maintenance on the aircraft that was required during the missions. One mission that stands out in my memory was the time we were flying from Goose Bay, Labrador, to Thule, Greenland. Just past the point of no return we lost #1 engine D.C. generator due to an overheat condition. I crawled out through the wing to #1 nacelle, opened the firewall door, and found the generator too hot to touch. I told the pilot to feather #1 and I would remove the generator. While I was waiting for the generator to cool down so I could work on it, the pilot called me on the intercom and told me #1 engine was picking up too much ice because it was not running. I took a large screwdriver and hammered it into the field windings and told the pilot to crank #1. As the engine started to turn, the generator shaft sheared allowing the engine to run without the generator turning. We were able to complete our mission with no further problems.

— Donald L. Davis

I graduated from Aviation Cadets during the spring of 1953. My first assignment was to Korea flying C-47s Air Evac and troop carrier. Upon my return from Korea I was assigned to the 28th Logistic Support Squadron (LSS) and the huge C-124C Globemaster. I was lucky in that I was sent TDY for C-124 transition school at West Palm Beach AFB in Florida. The transition was fairly easy and enjoyable. The C-124 was a well built and easy aircraft to fly. We called it an all weather aircraft, it flew at the level you hit all the weather.

The 28th LSS was assigned to the 3079th Special Operations Wing at Wright Patterson AFB at Dayton, Ohio. We had 12 aircraft and 12 crews and flew all over the world. Our primary mission was flying the very early, very large nuclear bombs to many bases overseas. The bombs and dolly weighed approximately 36,000 lbs. During one such mission I took off from Westover AFB, Massachusetts. on a hot summer day at max gross weight of 185,000 lbs. Number 3 engine started back firing severely during lift off. We shut the engine down and continued on three engines. We could only climb to 300 feet due to overheated engines, so we circled around a very tall TV transmission tower then landed on the same runway in the opposite direction at full gross weight. We had that 36,000 lb bomb on board. The cause of the failure—rebuilt spark plugs. Someone's suggestion to rebuild spark plugs and save the Air Force a few dollars. Bad decision. Each engine had 56 spark plugs used on 28 cylinders. Using rebuilt plugs could have caused us to crash in Springfield, Massachusetts, just to save a few dollars.

We had many very special and interesting missions as well. One was to go to Lockheed at Palmdale, California and load a new F-104 Starfighter complete except for the engine. We flew it to Bolling AFB in Washington, D.C. to be put on a flat bed truck in President Eisenhower's Inauguration Parade.

I have many fond memories of flying the C-124. I have been through a hail storm, been hit by lightning, been through severe turbulence, but Ol' Shakey came through it all. A little slow, but steady and reliable for 4000 hrs for me. I still love her greatly.

— Edward E. Hoerman, Major, USAF (Ret.)

Lockheed C-130 "Hercules"

To meet a US Air Force Tactical Air Command requirement for a medium-weight transport capable of operating in and out of unprepared landing strips, a design competition was launched in 1951. Lockheed won and the C-130 prototype flew in August 1954. The highwing airlifter was centered on a very spacious fuselage, with an access ramp at the rear that could be lowered in flight for air drops. Orders soared and the plane was in high-rate production for many years, resulting in the 1,900th unit delivered in 1988, with production continuing at three a month. At the beginning of 1990 the C-130 was still in production, and in service with the Air Forces of 61 countries. The first batch of 219 C-130As began to enter TAC service in December 1956, and was followed by 242 C-130Bs. Work began in 1961 on the E model for the Military Airlift Command, with 488 being built, and 297 H models with a more powerful engine for the USAF and the Navy, plus more than 500 for other countries. The C-130 has performed every mission possible for a transport plane, from cargo carrier to flying hospital, gunship, electronic warfare platform, and inflight-refueling tanker. The C-130 is the most successful military transport still flying in the world today.

Specifications:

Type:	Tactical Transport
Crew:	5; accommodation for 92 troops or 64 fully-equipped paratroops
Power Plant:	4 4,500 hp Allison T54-4-15 Turboprops
Length:	97 ft 9 in
Height:	38 ft 3 in
Weight:	175,000 lb.
Wing Span:	132 ft 7 in
Armament:	None
Cost:	N/A

Lockheed C-130B "Hercules" S/N 57-0526

1959:	Delivered to the USAF by Lockheed
29 Nov. 1960	Delivered 6515th OMS Edwards AFB, CA
31 May 1973	6594th Test Group, Hill AFB, UT
19 Jan. 1987	6514th Test Squadron, Hill AFB, UT
27 Jan. 1994	Turned over to the Hill Aerospace Museum
Total Flight time:	11,009.6 Hours

Convair/General Dynamics C-131D "Samaritan"

Acquired by the USAF for short to medium range transport of administrative personnel, it was a military version of the civilian Convair 340, itself an updated modification of the Convair 240. It was used by thirty-five airlines and by the armed forces of five nations. You will notice on the right side of the fuselage large stars denoting it was used by a military officer of general rank. The USAF, needing aircraft which could be used as flying classrooms for training navigators and radar technicians, ordered 40 of the aircraft, calling it the T-29. The USAF also liked the readily convertible interior, which could be arranged to seat 44 to 56 passengers. This aircraft is a 1951 model. The inside is nicely finished with chairs for passengers and space for conferences. This aircraft was formerly assigned to the Idaho State National Guard. This type of aircraft was assigned to HAFB in 1960.

Specifications:

Type:	Personnel transport trainer
Crew:	3
Engines:	2 P&W piston-prop, 2,400 hp each
Cruise:	268 mph
Wingspan:	105 ft 8 in
Length:	79 ft 2 in
Height:	27 ft 9 in
Weight:	45,000 lb.
Armament:	None
Cost:	$520,000

Convair/General Dynamics C-131D "Samaritan" S/N 55-300

17 Mar. 1955	Delivered to the USAF by Convair/General Dynamics
Mar. 1955	Assigned to the 2750th ABW (AMC) Wright-Patterson AFB, OH
Jun. 1975	Assigned to HQ Air National Guard, Andrews AFB. Washington, DC As part of the Presidential Fleet
Mar. 1977	Assigned To 124th Tactical Reconnaissance Group (ANG) Boise, ID
Jul. 1989	Dropped from USAF Inventory.
Aug. 1989	Assigned to the Hill Aerospace Museum.

Cessna O-2A "Super Skymaster"

When Cessna first built their Model 337, they had in mind an aircraft that would be inexpensive and simple to fly. It would have the advantage of twin engines, mounted in tandem with a tractor engine in front and a pusher in the rear. It featured twin engine safety and center-line flight (no pull to one side) if an engine was lost. It was marketed emphasizing that feature. It also had twin tail booms, dual controls, and retractable nose gear. It was offered to the civilian market in 1965 as the "Super Skymaster" with four to six passenger seats. The USAF, looking for a low cost, off the shelf replacement for the single engine Cessna O-1E "Bird Dog" acquired a military version of the 337. The twin-engine safety feature was especially valued by USAF crews flying the O-2A in Vietnam where one engine could be lost to enemy ground fire. It was used for visual reconnaissance and Forward Air Control (FAC) since it was capable of loitering above a target area for hours. Fighters such as the F-4, F-100, and F-105 were too fast and too fuel-hungry for such a task. After identifying a target, the crew of the O-2A would mark it with smoke rockets and then, coordinated the attack of the "fast movers." The latter made their high speed attacks and quickly returned to home base for more fuel and ordnance. The O-2A crew then reported visible target damage to the fighters. The O-2A had four wing pylons on which it could carry WP marking rockets and 7.62 mini-gun pods or other light ordnance. An O-2B model was equipped with loudspeakers and carried leaflets to be used for psychological warfare. This aircraft was a war bird and saw action on three bases in Vietnam from 1969-1972. Production ended in 1970. It was assigned to 6514th Training Squadron, HAFB, in January 1975.

Specifications:

Type:	Visual reconnaissance, forward air control
Crew:	2
Engines:	2 Continental 10-360 of 210 hp each
Wingspan:	38 ft 2 in
Length:	29 ft 9 in
Height:	9 ft 2 in
Weight:	4,630 lb.
Speed:	199 mph
Cost:	$92,000
Armament:	Rockets, flares, 7.62 mini-guns, light ordinance

Cessna O-2A "Super Skymaster" S/N 68-10853

Apr. 1969	Delivered to the USAF by Cessna Aircraft Corp. Wichita, KS
May 1969	To 504th Tactical Air Support Group (PAF) Nha Trang AB, Vietnam
Oct. 1969	Deployed to Cam Ranh Bay AB, Vietnam
Aug. 1971	To 19th Tactical Air Support Sq. Phan Raang AB, Vietnam
Dec. 1971	Deployed to Da Nang, RVN
Mar. 1972	To 366th Tactical Fighter Wing, DaNang AB, Vietnam
Jun. 1972	To 6498th Air Base Support Wing, DaNang AB, Vietnam
Oct. 1972	To Davis-Nonthan AFB, AZ for storage
Jan. 1973	To 110th Tactical Air Support Group (ANG) Kellogg Field, MI
Jan. 1975	To 163rd Fighter Interceptor Group Ontario, CA
Jan. 1983	To Air Force Flight Test Center (AF Systems Command), Edwards AFB, CA
Jun. 1983	To 6514th Test Sq. (AFSC) Hill AFB, UT
Sep. 1983	Redesignated GO-2A
Sep. 1984	Placed on inactive status, Hill AFB, UT
Oct. 1984	To Hill AFB Aerospace Museum

Cessna O-2s at Davis-Monthan

Lockheed P-38J "Lightning"

The XP-38 prototype first flew December 1938. It was 1942 before the first genuine operational P-38 appeared. It still had a number of undesirable characteristics, including a tricky handling aspect. Lockheed developed the first Model 422 with chin radiators, increased fuel capacity, and power-boosted ailerons. It then became a truly effective fighter. It was nicknamed Der gabelschwanz Teufel (The Fork-Tail Devil) by the Germans. There were 2,970 of the F models produced. The K was the next model, designed for high altitude. Only one was built and it was converted to the J. Next came the most important of all: the P-38L. It had the V-1710-111/113 engines, improved equipment, and a provisional rack for bombs carried in Christmas Tree style under the wings.

One of the most famous stories of the P-38 is that of the flying circus. Major Tom Lynch and 2nd Lt. Richard Bong teamed up in their P-38F Lightnings to terrorize the Japanese-held island in the Solomons. Lynch, in his Lightning #79, on 27 December 1942 became an ace. This opened the door for Bong and on 8 Jannuary 1943, he became America's leading ace.

Specifications:

Type:	Single seat fighter
Crew:	1
Engines:	2 1,425 hp Allison V-1710 111/113 inline, liquid cooled
Speed:	414 mph
Service ceiling:	44.000 ft
Range:	2,260 miles
Wingspan:	52 ft 0 in
Weight:	empty 12,780 lb.; max. take off weight 21,000 lb.
Height:	9 ft 10 in
Length:	37 ft 10 in
Cost:	$97,147
Armament:	1 20 mm cannon and four 50 cal. machine guns; provision for 3,200 lb. of bombs or 10 5-inch rockets.
Total produced:	9,395

Lockheed P-38J "Lightning" S/N 42-67638

23 Nov. 1943	Delivered to the USAAF by Lockheed Company, Burbank, CA
May 1944	Assigned to 11th Air Force, 343rd Fighter Group, 54th Fighter Squadron, in AK
Feb. 1945	Crash-landed on Buldir Island, AK; only 385 hours on the aircraft; Pilot 1st. Lt. Arthur W. Kidder, Jr.; on local test flight after 50 hour inspection; aircraft demilitarized after crash and later used as a ground target for other P-38s on air-to-ground gunnery training.
Aug. 1993	Air Force Heritage Foundation of Utah explores the feasibility of recovery of aircraft from the crash site.
Aug. 1994	AFHFOU recovered aircraft from the Aleutian Islands for restoration; Art Kidder, who crashed landed aircraft, assisted in the recovery.
Oct. 1994	Delivered to Kal Aero in CA for restoration.
Aug. 1996	Aircraft returned to Hill AFB and prepared for display.

Scarcely a WWII fighter pilot exists who cannot regale you with the numerous close calls he experienced in aerial combat. Few, however, can claim that the respect for their plane saved their life. Such is the case with Colonel Heber M. Butler (USAF, retired), who flew the P-38 during WWII. The USAAF had planned a three bomber group raid on Naples, Italy. The first bomber group consisted of B-26s, the second of B-25s, and finally the high-altitude B-17s would finish up. Each group was to be escorted by a fighter group of P-38s: the 82nd, 14th, and 1st.

"I was in the 82nd Fighter Group, 97th Squadron, and we were escorting the old B-26 Martin `Cigars,' that we hated to escort, because it was so slow," recalled Butler. "That plane would take off at 145 mph, climb at 145 mph, dive at 145 mph... and we'd sit back and try to keep up enough airspeed so that if the ME109s [German fighters] came in, we could turn into them." The plan called for 82nd to escort the B-26s out to sea and out of reach of the ME109s and then turn around and come back in and help with the second group of B-25s. Then when the two fighter groups escorted them off the target, they both went back in with the third group of B-17s. "By that time, there were three great big balls of fighters going round and round," explained Butler about the massive cloud of planes that he ended up in. "It was the biggest, hairiest dogfight I had ever seen!"

Following one more short dogfight, Butler emerged with no ammunition, and only a trace more in fuel. "I headed south for Sicily, because I knew I didn't have enough fuel left to get back to our base in Africa," reminisced Butler. "As I was on the deck heading south, I looked up and here is another ball of fighters going round and round. Well, there was no sense in me pulling up in there, I didn't have anything to shoot with. Then here come two P-38s in a big dive out of that fight, and one of them latched onto my right wing. I punched the radio button and said, `Keep your eyes open, I'm out of ammunition!' He said, `So am I!' Then the other guy slides in from the left, and said, `That makes three of us!' When we were about 20 miles south of the main, big fight, here comes seven ME109s at about 5,000 to 6,000 feet. They were coming in line-abreast formation, because they liked to peal off one at a time and come in a trail, one after another, with each one shooting at the same target. Pretty soon the first one started to roll in after us, and this kid on my right just hauled that P-38 up in a vertical climb and straight up at the 109. That 109 whopped back up in his formation and all seven of them kept going."

When asked if the German's respect for the P-38 was responsible for saving his life, Butler answered with an emphatic "Yes!" "They didn't like to make a nose on pass, because if you do, and that P-38 gets into you with those four parallel firing 50s and the 20 mm, you just blow up! They knew that... and yes, it saved our lives-all three of us!"

North American P-51 "Mustang"

One of the greatest fighters of WWII, it was one of the very few aircraft type that was conceived during the hostilities to see large scale service. The P-51 was originally designed as a short range fighter to re-equip RAF Spitfire and Hurricane squadrons depleted during the "Battle of Britain." A 120-day limit was imposed on North American to build a prototype and they delivered one in 117 days. The P-51 first flew in October 1940 and the first production models were delivered a year later to the RAF who christened it the "Mustang." Early on, it was obvious an improved engine was needed to achieve greater high altitude performance. A Rolls-Royce Merlin engine was installed and from then on the P-51 never looked back. Design improvements in 1942 increased the maximum speed from 390 MPH to 441 MPH at optimum altitude. Delivery to the 8th AF began on 1 December 1943. It flew its first combat mission 12 days later. It had a range of 2080 miles with the use of wing tanks. It could fly far in excess of other fighters of the day. In 1944 they began to fly escort missions with the B-17's and B-24's to their targets over Berlin. Our aircraft is painted in the colors of Col. Chesley Peterson's 4th fighter Group of the 8th AF.

The P-51 went on to serve in Korea and many survived as the Cavalier F-51D, a tactical fighter, until the late 1960s. Many are around today as civilian sport models. Hill AFB was responsible for storage and repair of the P-51 until 1947.

Specifications:

Type:	Single seat fighter
Crew:	1
Power Plant:	1 1,380 hp V-1650-9 (R/R Merlin 1695 hp)
Wingspan:	37 ft 0 in
Length:	33 ft 4 in
Height:	13 ft 8 in
Weight:	Empty 6,585 lb.; Gross 11,054 lb.
Cost:	$51,572
Speed:	max. 487 mph; cruising speed 380 mph
Range:	850 miles (2,080 with drop tanks)
Total produced:	15,686

North American P-51 "Mustang" S/N 44-13371

Project title:	1940 NA-73X
26 Oct. 1940	First flight
1 May 1941	Designated Mustang MK 1
Sep. 1942-Mar. 1943	USAAF designated A-36
1943	An experiments began to upgrade with the Rolls-Royce Merlin 61 engine
1 Dec. 1943	First service with 8th AF England
1944	D Model introduced
1993	Acquired by the Hill Aerospace Museum

Our P-51 here at the Hill Aerospace Museum is re-constructed and painted in the colors of Col. Chesley Peterson's 4th Fighter Group of the 8th Air Force. It is named after Col. Peterson's wife, Audry Boyes Peterson. This aircraft is one of those purchased by the Foundation and donated to the Museum.

P-51s flying in formation—"Little Friends"

P-51 Mustang

Probably the greatest propeller-driven fighter of WWII, it was one of the very few aircraft conceived during the hostilities that saw large-scale service. The P-51 was originally designed as a long-range addition to the depleted RAF fighter squadrons. A 120-day limit was imposed on North American to build a prototype and they delivered it in 117 days. The P-51 first flew in October 1940 as the NA-73X. The first production models (AG-345) were delivered to the RAF who christened them the Mustang I. Below 12,000 ft. with an Allison engine, the airplane performed as expected, but at altitudes above that, performance fell drastically. In 1942 the British installed a Rolls Royce Merlin engine, which increased speed from 390 to 441 mph.

The United States Army Air Corps at first designated the aircraft as the Apache (A-36) in late 1941. Its first service came in Tunisia on April 9, 1943, as an attack aircraft.

In the summer of 1942 the airframe was mated with a Packard built V-1650-3 Merlin engine and a four-bladed Hamilton Standard propeller. This provided 50 mph more speed and a 10,000 ft. ceiling increase. The P-51C (identical to the P-51B) was built at the Dallas, Texas plant. The first combat with the new models came December 1, 1943. Both models were given a new V-1650-7 engine. Three thousand seven hundred thirty-eight B/C models were built.

As aircraft numbers increased, they accompanied B-17s and B-24s on long-range missions over German targets. By the middle of 1944, they had virtually eliminated the German Air Force as a threat. Early in 1944 the D model was introduced with a bubble canopy and an improved supercharger, which increased performance. The number of guns was increased to six. Nine thousand six hundred three D models were built.

Chesley Gordon Peterson: A Utah Hero

Major General Chesley Gordon Peterson became one of the finest fighter pilots of World War II. Born on August 10, 1920, in Salmon, Idaho, he attended school in Santaquin, Utah, and later at BYU. His fascination with airplanes and flying stemmed from an early age when he was captivated by barnstormers performing in the skies above Utah County. In 1939 he entered the U.S. Army Air Corps as a cadet, but before he completed his training, it was discovered that he had misrepresented his age with a forged birth certificate, and was actually too young to be a pilot. Instead of court-marshaling Peterson, the board stated that he was dismissed "for lack of inherent flying ability." While working at Douglas Aircraft in Los Angeles, he met Colonel Charles Sweeney, who recruited Peterson for the Royal Air Force. Peterson arrived at Church Fenton, England, in late 1940 as a volunteer for the Eagle Squadron — a group of foreign volunteers that would fly RAF Hawker Hurricanes and Spitfires against the German Luftwaffe. At the age of 21, Peterson became the first American to command the 71st Eagle Squadron. He completed 42 missions for the RAF, was promoted to the rank of Flight Lieutenant, and was awarded the RAF Distinguished Flying Cross.

In 1942, when the United States entered the war, Peterson transferred to U.S. forces, along with the Eagle Squadron, and took over command of the 4th Fighter Group in England as a Major in the U.S. Army. He was later promoted to the rank of Colonel at age 23, the youngest full Colonel in U.S. Army Air Corps history. During WWII he flew about 130 combat missions and became an "ace" by downing nine German airplanes, with another nine probable kills. Peterson even survived a 500-foot fall into the English Channel when his parachute failed to open after bailing out of a disabled P-47 Thunderbolt. Peterson was the first American fighter pilot to win both the U.S. Distinguished Service Cross and Britain's Distinguished Service Order — each country's second-highest military decoration. He also was awarded the Distinguished Flying Cross, five U.S. Air Medals, and the Purple Heart.

After the war, Peterson rose to the rank of Major General, serving in various capacities around the world. He was a member of the U.S. Military and Air Attaché to South Africa, Commander of the 48th Fighter Bomber Wing at Chaumont, France, Director of Intelligence with the U.S. Strike Command at MacDill AFB, Florida, and on the staff of the Commander in Chief of Pacific Air Forces. Major General Peterson retired from the Air Force on Aug. 1, 1970, at the age of 49. He lived in Ogden, Utah, then later moved to the Air Force retirement village at March AFB in Riverside, CA. He died at the age of 69 on January 28, 1990, and was buried with full military honors at Riverside National Cemetery.

Chesley Peterson (third from right) walking with aircrew

Curtiss P-40 "Warhawk"

After evaluation trials in May 1939 in competition with other pursuit prototypes, the XP-40 was declared the most acceptable, and an order for 524 P-40s was placed. Production continued with the P-40B, similar to the British Tomahawk II. The P-40B introduced armor protection for the pilot and doubled the wing firepower from two to four .30 cal. machine guns, in addition to two .50 cal. guns mounted on the engine cowling. Curtiss built 131 P-40Bs in 1941 before going over to P-40C production which had improved self sealing fuel tanks. On 7 December 1941, a few P-40s managed to get into the air at Pearl Harbor and joined in scoring the first American fighter kills on Japanese aircraft. Although short on performance compared with other American Fighters in service at the out-break of war, the P-40 was available in large numbers with highly trained pilots to fly them. It earned its fame through the activities of less than 100 aircraft flying in China with the American Volunteer Group, the "Flying Tigers" commanded by General Claire Chennault. Operating in a hostile environment using equipment inferior to the enemy, the P-40s with their red and white teeth emblems on the nose, went into combat two weeks after Pearl Harbor and, before being disbanded in 1942, shot down 286 Japanese aircraft with the loss of only eight. Curtiss produced 13,783 P-40s in various configurations, known as the Warhawk, Kittyhawk, and the Tomahawk. These fighters served throughout the war on every front with no less than 28 Allied Nations. No other fighter during the war saw wider service. In the winter of 1941-1942 Hill AFB had the responsibility for overhaul of the P-40. On 26 August 1944 a production line was set up for the storage of various aircraft. Hill stored 250 operational ready P-40s during WWII.

S/N Unknown. This aircraft not available at this time—being restored in California.

Specifications:

Type:	Single-seat pursuit, ground attack, reconnaissance, and advanced trainer
Crew:	1
Power plant:	1 1,360 hp
Length:	33 ft 4 in
Height:	12 ft 4 in
Weight:	8,850 lb.
Wing span:	37 ft 4 in
Armament:	6 .50 in guns, one 500 lb. bomb
Total produced:	13,783
Cost:	N/A

North American T-28 "Trojan"

The prototype for the Trojan T-28 won the 1948 USAF design competition to replace the Texan (AT-6). The T-28 was test flown on 26 September 1949 and then ordered by the US Navy in 1952 as part of the US Forces standardization program. Hill AFB had a Storage Mission on a large number of aircraft and the T-28 was one of these. The T-28 began to be phased out in July 1957 and was completely dropped from the inventory by June of 1958.

Specifications:

Type:	Trainer
Power Plant:	1 800 hp RP1300-1
Wing Span:	40 ft 1 in
Length:	32 ft
Height:	12 ft 8 in
Weight:	8,495 lb. gross
Speed:	380 mph
Armament:	None
Cost:	N/A

North American T-28 "Trojan" S/N 137749

2 May 1954	Accepted by USAF at Inglewood, CA
7 Jun. 1954	To Corpus Cristi NAS
14 Jun. 1954	To Kingville NAS
9 Nov. 1961	To Pensacola NAS
4 Jan. 1969	To Cecil Field NAS
8 May 1969	To Davis-Monthan AFB
24 Feb. 1970	To Pensacola NAS
29 Feb. 1972	To LeMoore NAS
12 Jan. 1973	To Whiting Field NAS
12 Jun. 1976	To Pensacola NAS
5 Dec. 1978	To Corpus Cristi NAS
12 Sep. 1980	To Pensacola NAS
3 Jun. 1981	To Corpus Cristi
24 Nov. 1982	To Pensacola NAS
23 Feb. 1983	To Corpus Cristi NAS
27 Feb. 1984	To Pensacola NAS
12 Jul. 1988	To Davis-Monthan AFB and on to the Hill Aerospace Museum

Total flight time	18,107 hours

T-28 on taxiway with the canopies open

Cessna U-3A (L27A) "Blue Canoe"

In the mid-1950s the USAF initiated a competition to select a suitable off-the-shelf design to serve as an administrative liaison and cargo utility aircraft. Cessna presented its popular 310 model, which was accepted with slight modifications. This aircraft first flew on 3 January 1953. An interesting aspect of the aircraft was that all fuel was carried in the wing tanks. Later models, such as the Turbo-system Skyknight, sometimes known as the Model 320, had individual seats, air conditioning, and an oxygen system. The USAF acquired 160 U-3As. The Cessna model 310 continued in production for more than twenty-five years, indicating its popularity with the flying public. A small number served with the French Air Force. This aircraft was assigned to HAFB in 1960.

Specifications:

Type:	Administrative Liaison, utility cargo
Engines:	2 Continental flat, 260 hp
Crew:	2 + 2 passengers
Wing span:	35 ft 9 in
Speed:	236 mph max.; cruise 220 mph
Wingspan:	35 ft 9 in
Length:	29 ft 7 in
Weight:	5,300 lb.
Height:	9 ft 11 1/4 in
Cost:	N/A
Armament:	None

Cessna U-3A (L27A) "Blue Canoe" S/N 42-90406

29 Jul. 1957	Delivered to USAF by Cessna Aircraft Corp, Wichita, KS
Jul. 1957	To 4080th Air Base Group (SAC) Laughlin AFB, TX
Oct. 1958	Redesignated U-3A
May 1959	To 4080th Combat Support Group (SAC) Laughlin AFB, TX
May 1961	To 4080th Strategic Wing (SAC) Laughlin AFB, TX
Unknown:	Deployed to Davis-Monthan AFB, AZ
Oct. 1966	To East Coast Flying Service, Imeson Airport, Jacksonville, FL
Dec. 1966	To 100th Strategic Wing (SAC) Davis-Monthan AFB, AZ
Oct. 1968	To 161st Aeromedical Evacuation Group (ANG) Sky Harbor Airport, Phoenix, AZ
Jun. 1969	To 111th Tactical Support Group (ANG) Willow Grove Naval Air Station, PA
Mar. 1971	To 104th Tactical Fighter Group (ANG) Barnes Field, Westfield, MA
Jun. 1972	Dropped from the USAF inventory
May 1980	Donated to USAF by TSARCOM, St. Louis, MO
Jun. 1988	To Hill AFB Aerospace Museum

Convair T-29 "Samaritan"

The T-29 was purchased by the USAF for training and transportation, and was first flown on 22 September 1949. The manufacturer was the Convair Division of General Dynamics Corporation. The USAF, needing aircraft which could be used as flying classrooms for training navigators and radar technicians, ordered 40 of the aircraft, which were called the T-29. On this aircraft, ten persons had access to facilities for training as navigators and four as radar technicians. This model was unpressurized, so an oxygen outlet was provided for each trainee position. A later B model was pressurized. Hill AFB had one T-29 assigned until the late 1960s.

Specifications:

Type:	Navigator-bombardier trainer
Crew:	2
Engines:	2 1864-KW P&W R-2800-99W 2,400 hp each
Wing Span:	105 ft 4 in
Weight:	47,000 lb.
Length:	79 ft 2 in
Height:	28 ft 2 in
Armament:	None

Convair T-29 "Samaritan" S/N 52-1119

13 Jan. 1954	Delivered to the USAF by Consolidated-Vultee, San Diego, CA
Jan. 1954	To 3610th Observer Training Wing (ATC) Harlingen AFB, TX
May 1955	To 3610th Aircraft Observer Trng. Wing (ATC) Harlingen, TX
Sep. 1956	To 3610 Navigator Training Wing (ATC) Harlingen AFB, TX
Jan. 1958	To 7625th Operations Sq. (USAF Academy) Lowry AFB, CO
May 1960	To 3610th Navigator Training Sq. (ATC) Harlingen AFB, TX
Jul. 1962	To 3565 Maintenance and Supply Grp. (ATC) Connally AFB, TX
Apr. 1966	To 3535th Navigator Training Wing (ATC) Mather AFB, CA
Feb. 1975	Dropped From Inventory
Spring 1992	Delivered to the Hill Aerospace Museum for display

Fairchild A-10 "Thunderbolt II"

The first prototype flew on 10 May 1972, and the first pre-production aircraft flew on 15 February 1975. The first production aircraft was flown on 21 October 1975. Piston-engined aircraft such as the single-seat Mustang and the F-82 Twin Mustang (in the Korean Conflict) and the Douglas A-1 Skyraiders (in Vietnam) proved highly unsuccessful in a predominantly jet environment. Experience gained in both Korea and Vietnam prompted the need for a modern equivalent. What was needed was a close-air-support aircraft with heavy payload, good endurance, and heavy battle damage resistant. The A-10 is the first USAF aircraft developed specifically to deliver aerial firepower to defeat enemy ground targets. The pilot is protected by a titanium armor-plated "bathtub," which also protects the vital elements of the flight control system. It is claimed that the A-10 can lose one engine, half a tail, two-thirds of the wing, and parts of the fuselage and still remain airborne. The A-10 is also nicknamed the "Flying Can Opener."

Specifications:

Type:	Close air support
Crew:	1
Engines:	2 GE TF-34-GE-100 turbofans, 9,065 lb. thrust ea.
Wing Span:	57 ft 6 in
Height:	14 ft 8 in
Speed:	439 mph
Cruising:	387 mph
Length:	53 ft 4 in
Armament:	1 7-barrel 30 mm General Electric GAU-8 Avenger rotary cannon; 11 external stations for a max. of 9,540 lb. ordnance (with full internal fuel and 1170 lb. 30 mm ammunition).
Cost:	N/A

Fairchild Republic A-10A "Thunderbolt II" S/N 73-1666

24 Jun. 1975	Delivered to USAF by Fairchild Republic, Hagerstown, MD
Jun. 1975	To Edwards AFB, CA
Mar. 1980	To Air Force Flight TestCenter (AF Systems Command), Edwards AFB (to YA-10A)
Mar. 1985	To AF Armament Development Test Center (AFSC) Eglin AFB, FL
Sep. 1989	To 3246th Test Wing (AFSC) Eglin AFB, FL
Jan. 1990	To Sheppard Technical Training Center (Air Training Command (Sheppard AFB, TX) to GYA-10A ground instructional airframe
Mar. 1992	To HAFB Museum

Boeing B-52G "Stratofortress"

The B-52 was dubbed the BUFF (Big Ugly Fat "Fellow"). It was used in Southeast Asia and Desert Storm as a long range Tactical Bomber. It could attack both Tactical and Interdiction targets. Striking silently from high altitude it produced devastating physical and psychological effect on the enemy units. Its mission in Vietnam was one of the paradoxes of the war. The mighty earth girdling bomber became the most feared of all Tactical Weapons. It operated from bases on Guam and U-Tapao, Thailand. Between 1968 and 1971 it flew about 1000 to 1800 sorties a month. The last B-52G was produced in late 1960 and was later replaced with the H models. The 456th Bombardment Wing (Det.1) was activated at Hill on 1 January 1973 and on 28 December 1973 the first of four B-52s arrived at the base. They flew training missions until 1 July 1975 when the unit was deactivated.

Specifications:

Type:	Long-range heavy Bomber and cruise missile carrier
Power Plant:	8 Pratt & Whitney J-57-P-43 turbojet
Wingspan:	185 ft
Length:	157 ft 6 7/8 in
Height:	40 ft 8 in
Speed:	665 MPH
Max. Ceiling:	59,000 ft
Weight:	Max. load 488,000 lb.
Cost:	$7,000,000

Boeing B-52G-100 "Stratofortress" S/N 58-101

16 Oct. 1959	Delivered to USAF by Boeing Aircraft Corp. Wichita, KS
Oct. 1959	To 72nd Bombardment (Heavy) SAC, Ramey AFB, PR (Deployed to Biggs AFB, TX)
May 1962	To Boeing at Wichita, KS
Jul. 1963	To 456th Bombardment (H) Beale AFB, CA (Deployed to Anderson AFB, Guam)
Jan. 1973	To 17th Bombardment (H) Wing (SAC) Anderson AFB, Guam
Oct. 1973	To Robins AFB, GA
May 1974	To 2nd Bombardment (H) Wing (SAC) Barksdale AFB, LA
Nov. 1974	To 320th Bombardment (H) Wing (SAC) Mather AFB, CA
Jun. 1975	To 97th Bombardment (H) Wing (SAC) Blytheville AFB, AR (Deployed to Edwards AFB, CA)
Sep. 1983	To 62nd Bombardment (H) Wing (SAC) Fairchild AFB, WA
Feb. 1984	To 93rd Bombardment (H) Wing (SAC) Castle AFB, CA
Feb. 1987	To 2nd Bombardment (H) Wing (SAC) Barksdale AFB, LA
Dec. 1988	To 93rd Bombardment (H) Wing (SAC) Castle AFB, CA
Aug. 1991	To Hill Aerospace Museum Hill AFB, UT for display.

B-52 in flight with Skybolt missiles

Martin B-57A "Canberra"

There's more to this aircraft than immediately meets the eye. High performance is the key word. Designed and built in 1951 by the British Electric Company, it was called the "Canberra." Two were flown non-stop across the Atlantic Ocean setting a new world speed record. The philosophy of having no defensive armament was the result of experience with the famous DeHavilland-built Mosquito bomber: it's better to show the enemy a clean pair of heels than to stay around and try to fight him. The American Martin Aircraft Co. immediately bought the rights to test and build it as the B-57A. It was very versatile, being flown during the cold war and in Vietnam for tactical bombing, strafing, high altitude day photo reconnaissance, night reconnaissance, and as an early warning platform. It was the first foreign designed aircraft to be used by the USAF. General Dynamics Corporation modified 21 aircraft designating them the RB-57F. The modification included long drooping wings (122 ft. span), and a bulbous nose. In addition, two small jet engines (J-60s) were added for fuel economy. The larger engines were shut down while cruising at altitudes above 105,000 ft. NASA used one, (now on display at Pima County Air Museum in Arizona) for studying curvature of the earth from high altitude. Ideas taken from those aircraft were included in the design of Lockheed's famous U-2. Fuel economy, high altitude operation, and mission diversity made it a valuable aircraft for the USAF. The two-man crew sit side by side, and if needed, a third crew member may be added. The bomb bay, with doors that rotated up into the fuselage, carried 5,000 lb. of bombs. Eight rockets were carried on pylons under the wings. The large orange pods on the wing tips carried extra fuel. Our aircraft was obtained for the Museum in 1990. The B-57 became America's first jet-powered medium bomber.

Specifications:

Type:	Tactical bomber, photo and recon
Crew:	2-3
Engine:	2 Wright J-65 of 7,000 lb. thrust ea.
Cruise:	450 mph
Wingspan:	64 ft
Length:	65 ft 6 in
Height:	15 ft 6 in
Weight:	54,950 lb.
Armament:	4 20mm cannon or 8 .50 cal. guns + 5,000 lb. ordnance
Cost:	$1,071,000

Martin B-57A "Canberra" S/N 52-1492

1 Nov. 1954	Delivered to USAF by Glen Martin Co. Under license to English Electric Co.
Oct. 1954	To Martin/Baltimore via Warner-Robbins Air Material Center, Robbins AFB, GA
Sep. 1955	To 7499th Support Group (US Air Forces in Europe), Wiesbaden AB, Germany
Feb. 1956	To 7407th Support Sq. (USAFE), Rhein-Mein AB, Germany
Nov. 1959	To Air Material Command Headquarters, (AMC),Wright Patterson AFB, OH
Mar. 1960	To 7407th Support Sq. (USAFE), Rhein-Mein AB, Germany
Dec. 1960	To 4440th Aircraft Delivery Group (TAC) Langley AFB, VA
Dec. 1960	To Air Force Logistics Command Headquarters, Wright Patterson AFB, OH and dropped from USAF inventory.
Dec. 1990	Reassembled at Hill AFB for display at Museum

B-57 at HAFB with starting cartridge smoke

Lockheed C-140 "Jetstar"

Designed initially to meet a military requirement for a medium-weight, multi-engined jet utility transport and trainer, the Jetstar was also developed into a business executive aircraft. The first production aircraft flew in the summer of 1960. The sixth aircraft, the first for a commercial customer, was delivered early in 1961 to the Continental Can Company. Sixteen C-140s were produced for the USAF. Five Jetstars were used by the Air Force Airways and Air Communications Service to inspect worldwide military navigation aids. They had complete airliner appointments including automatic oxygen mask delivery in case of loss of cabin pressure. These have large slipper type fuel tanks attached to the wings. Six aircraft went to the Airlift Command, and five others were delivered to USAFE operational support units. Production stopped in 1981. Hill AFB had one assigned with the AFCC.

Specifications:

Type:	Executive and Utility Transport
Crew:	2 - 3
Power Plant:	4 Pratt & Whitney JT12A-6 Single Shaft Turbojets
Wingspan:	54 ft 5 in
Length:	60 ft 5 in
Height:	20 ft 6 in
Weight:	40,920 lb.
Speed:	550 mph at 45,000 ft
Cost:	N/A
Range:	2280 miles
Armament:	None

Lockheed C140B "Jetstar" S/N 62-4201

3 Jul. 1963	Delivered to USAF by Lockheed, Marietta, GA
Jul. 1963	To 1254th Air Transport Wing, Special Mission (MATS) Andrews AFB, MD
Jan. 1966	To 89th Military Airlift Wing, Special Mission (MATS) Andrews AFB, MD
Jan. 1972	Redesignated VC-140B
Jul. 1977	To 435th Tactical Airlift Wing (MAC) Ramstein AB, Germany
Feb. 1978	Redesignated C-140B
Jun. 1978	To 58th Military Airlift Sq. (MAC) Ramstein AB, Germany
Mar. 1982	To 89th Military Airlift Wing, Special Mission (MAC) Andrews AFB, MD
Jan. 1987	To 58th Military Airlift Sq. (MAC), Ramstein AB, Germany
Oct. 1987	To 379th Aeromedical Airlift Wing, (MAC), Scott AFB, IL
Oct. 1987	To 1467th Facilities Checking Sq. (MAC), Scott AFB, IL
Jan. 1989	To Davis-Monthan AFB, AZ as excess; dropped from inventory
Jan. 1992	To Hill Aerospace Museum

C-140 in Presidential fleet colors

McDonnell-Douglas F-4C "Phantom II"

This versatile aircraft was in service with the USAF, US Navy, and eleven other countries. It has been called the most significant and successful aircraft of the 1960s. In the 1973 "Yom Kippur War," the Israelis called it the "Hammer." Furthermore, its history is not yet complete because it continues to serve the U.S. and other nations around the world. Design began for the US Navy in 1952. Innovations eventually included "fly-by-wire," negative slant of the stabilator, automatic variable air intakes for engine efficiency, and leading-edge flaps. In 1963 the USAF began acquiring the aircraft for use in interception, air superiority bombing, close air support, and Wild Weasel "SAM" suppression. It was fast, rugged, agile, stable, and handled well. It could carry eleven tons of ordnance as well as air-to-air missiles. It exceeded the expectations of its designers and became the USAF's number one airplane. It set an altitude record of 98,557 ft, a speed record of 1,606 mph, and could climb at a 70-degree angle. HAFB was responsible for depot maintenance beginning in 1964, as well as for supply support until the early 1990s.

Specifications:

Type:	Fighter-bomber
Crew:	2
Wingspan:	38 ft 4 in
Length:	63 ft
Height:	16 ft 6 in
Weight:	58,000 lb.
Speed:	max. 1,450 mph; cruise 590
Cost:	$2,481,000
Armament:	1 GE M61AL 20mm rotary cannon + up to 11 tons ordnance
Power Plant:	2 GE J-79's at 17,000 lb. thrust each

McDonnell-Douglas F-4C "Phantom II" S/N 63-7424

3 Feb. 1964	Delivered to USAF by McDonnell-Douglas, St. Louis, MO
5 Feb. 1964	Crashed with 14 flying hours
Jun. 1964	Trucked to Hill AFB, to become the first F-4 to go through Hill's Crash Damage Program
Mar. 1966	Test flown, following the flight it took the life of an aircraft mechanic in a ground accident.
Oct. 1983	To National Aeronautics and Space Administration, Edwards AFB, CA
Aug. 1985	Returned to Ogden ALC
Dec. 1989	To Hill Aerospace Museum

The F-4C "424" in the Museum inventory has an interesting history, according to its crew chief Larry Bell, a Museum volunteer and former System Manager at Hill AFB with 21 years experience in the F-4 Phantom. "The plane came out of McDonnell Douglas and was received by the Air Force after the usual acceptance flight. It was then flown straight to Hill Field for modification. From Hill it was ferried to Mountain Home AFB and landed safely, but when a ground crewman went out to ground the aircraft as it was parked on the flightline, static electricity caused an arc which resulted in the aircraft burning right there on the ramp. The Combat Logistics Support Squadron came out and crated the plane up and shipped it back to Hill. It ended up being one of the first F-4s to be put through the Crash Damage Repair line at Hill. After it was completely rebuilt it was moved over to the Area Support Group as a test airplane. It stayed in Air Force Materiel Command and never went back to Tactical Air Command. Special wiring, instrumentation, and antennas were installed for flight test operations at the base."

But the plane's unusual history didn't end there. "One day a maintenance technician was conducting a preflight checkout of the plane out on the flightline next to Building 219. He had stepped over into the cockpit to run the canopy down and watch the linkage to make sure it locked properly, but he didn't sit down in the seat. He stepped into the ejection seat and squatted down low enough for the canopy to clear, then reached over and hit the canopy switch. When the canopy came down, the ejection seat accidentally fired and the technician was killed instantly."

The luckless F-4C went on to fly again though. In fact, "424" was flown in countless flight tests out over the Utah Test and Training Range west of Hill AFB, including many munitions tests. In October 1983 the aircraft was assigned to NASA at Edward's AFB for flight test operations. It returned to Ogden ALC on 29 August 1985 to continue flight test support here. "424" was finally retired and assigned to Hill Aerospace Museum in December 1989.

The first F-4C at Hill

McDonnell-Douglas RF-4C "Phantom II"

Developed to replace the RF-101. The RF-4C is a multisensor reconnaissance version of the F-4B "Phantom II". The first production model flew in May 1964, and 505 were built before manufacture ended in December 1973. They were operated by TAC, PACAF, and USAFE tactical reconnaissance units, and by units of the ANG. Radar and photographic systems are housed in the modified nose, increasing the overall length of the aircraft 4 ft. 8 in. The missile control system was deleted. The reconnaissance systems was installed which operated from the rear seat. (1) It included forward-looking radar with terrain following and avoidance modes, comprehensive array of cameras in the nose. (2) High and low altitude panoramic camera with optical viewfinders in the front cockpit. (3) Side-looking airborne radar (SLAR). (4) Infrared detection line scanner, and Tactical Electronic reconnaissance system.

Specifications:

Type:	Reconnaissance Fighter
Crew:	2
Power Plant:	2 J-79-GE-17's at 17,000 lb. thrust each
Wingspan:	38 ft 4 in
Length:	65 ft 9 in
Height:	16 ft 6 in
Weight:	58,000 lb.
Speed:	1,450 mph
Cruise:	590 mph
Armament:	Later versions carried the sidewinder
Cost:	$2,481,000 plus

McDonnell Douglas RF-4C "Phantom II" S/N 66-0469

30 Oct. 1967	Delivered to USAF by McDonnell Douglas Aircraft Corp. St. Louis, MO
Nov. 1967	To Bergstrom AFB, TX
Feb. 1968	To 75th Training Wing, Bergstrom AFB, TX
Jul. 1968	To Ogden ALC, HAFB, UT
Mar. 1970	To Bergstrom AFB, TX
Dec. 1970	To Wright Patterson AFB, OH
Oct. 1971	To Tactical Air Command, Eglin AFB, FL
Oct. 1972	To Ogden ALC, HAFB, UT
Dec. 1972	To Bergstrom AFB, TX
Oct. 1973	To Ogden ALC, HAFB, UT
Feb. 1974	To 67th Training Wing Bergstrom AFB, TX
Oct. 1975	To Ogden ALC, HAFB, UT
Oct. 1975	To Shaw AFB, SC
Jun. 1978	To Ogden ALC, HAFB, UT
Aug. 1982	To Bergstrom AFB, TX
Jan. 1983	To Ogden ALC, HAFB, UT
Jun. 1983	4467th Training Wing, Bergstrom AFB, TX
Aug. 1985	To Ogden ALC, HAFB, UT
Dec. 1991	To Ogden ALC, HAFB, UT
31 Jan. 1994	Declared Surplus
Oct. 1994	To Hill Aerospace Museum, HAFB, UT

An RF-4C on the flightline at HAFB

Lockheed F-80A "Shooting Star"

The first all-jet aircraft to be used operationally by the United States Air Force, was the P-80A "Shooting Star." It was conceptually ahead of other jet aircraft of its time, and faster by 100 to 150 mph than our propeller driven fighters. Design began in August 1943 by the design genius Kelly Johnson and his team at the "Lockheed Skunk Works." It first flew on 9 January 1944. Engine problems held up further flights until 10 June 1944. It featured hydraulic boost tail surfaces, fuselage mounted speed brakes, and a detachable after-fuselage for engine repair. It set a world airspeed record on 19 June 1947 at 623.8 mph. The P-80 was not ready for service when WWII ended. However some were in England by January 1945. It was outclassed by the MiG-15's in the Korean War. Lt. Russell Brown shot down the first MiG-15 in the first clash between pure jet aircraft of the Korean War. It was used for reconnaissance, close air support, as a fighter-bomber (being among the first to drop napalm), and training. Its most enduring variant is the well known T-33 "T-Bird." The P-80A was redesignated the F-80A in June 1948. Ogden Air Material Area was a storage location for the F-80 in 1952, and in 1963 was given engine repair responsibility.

Specifications:

Type:	Fighter-bomber
Crew:	1
Wingspan:	38 ft 10 in
Length:	34 ft 6 in
Height:	11 ft 4 in
Weight:	14,000 lb.
Engine:	GE J-33 3,850 lb. thrust
Range:	780 miles
Speed:	558 mph at S.L.
Total produced:	1,728
Armament:	6 .50 cal. guns & 1 ton bombs
Cost:	N/A

Lockheed F-80A "Shooting Star" S/N 44-84999

AERO NOSTALGIA located in Stockton, California re-constructed a USAF Lockheed T-33 to an F-80 configuration for display at the Hill Air Force Base Museum.

The F-80, was based upon an airframe which rolled onto the Aero Nostalgia hanger as a severely derelict T-33A found in a park in Florida. Because the T-33 retains identical components of the F-80 design, it was a fairly straight forward process to make the airframe resemble the F-80. They selected a paint scheme for the F-80, which was painted as F-80A S/N 44-84999. This machine was built by Lockheed as a P-80A and the Army Air Force accepted it for service on 30 April, 1945. It served in several units through its five years of duty which ended in October 1950 when it was withdrawn from use. When it was finished it was disassembled and trucked to the Museum. Upon arrival it was quickly reassembled and placed on display at the Museum.

F-80 flying in the clouds

Republic F-84F "Thunderstreak"

The phenomenal success of North American Aviation's F-86 "Sabre" encouraged Republic aircraft to proceed with a swept wing design of their own. Though design begun in 1949, problems of forging airframe members and matching a suitable engine to the airframe held up delivery until 1954. The F-84F was assigned the role of ground support fighter-bomber. It carried 6,000 pounds of bombs externally. The F-84F was used in the Suez War in 1956 and in the Greek-Turkish War in the mid-1960s. It was used by several NATO countries and was replaced by the supersonic F-100 in the USAF and assigned to Air National Guard Units in the late 1950s. The F-84Fs were recalled to active service during the Berlin Crisis in 1960 and assigned to Toul Rosiere Air Base in France. The RF84F (Reconnaissance-Fighter) model was designed with cameras in the nose, and air intakes at the wing roots. This particular aircraft saw active duty until 1965. It was assigned to the Air National Guard at Barnes Field in Massachusetts until dropped from the USAF inventory in 1972.

Specifications:

Type:	Subsonic fighter, tactical fighter bomber
Crew:	1
Wingspan:	33 ft 7 in
Length:	43 ft
Height:	14 ft 5 in
Weight:	27,000 lb.
Engine:	Wright J-65 of 7220 lb. thrust
Speed:	695 mph
Cost:	$769,999
Armament:	6 .50 cal. machine-guns + 6,000 lb. ordnance

Republic F-84F "Thunderstreak" S/N 51-1640

31 Dec. 1954	Delivered to the USAF by Republic Aviation, Farmingdale, NY
Jan. 1955	To 401st Fighter Bomber Grp. (TAC) Alexandria AFB, LA
Mar. 1956	To 3600th Combat Crew Training Wing (ATC) Luke AFB, AZ
Apr. 1956	To 401st Fighter Bomber Grp. (TAC) Alexandria AFB, LA
Jul. 1957	To 110th Fighter Interceptor Sq. (ANG) St. Louis, MO
Nov. 1961	Unit moved to TOUL ROSIERE AB, France (USAF)
Jul. 1962	To 12th Fighter Wing (TAC) Macdill AFB, FL
Oct. 1963	To 36th Tactical Fighter Wing (TAC) Holloman AFB, NM
Apr. 1965	To 104th Tactical Fighter Grp. (ANG) Barnes Field, MA
Aug. 1971	To Davis-Monthan AFB, AZ for storage
Apr. 1972	Dropped from USAF inventory
Mar. 1983	To Hill Aerospace Museum for Display

F-84F assembly line at Hill

Republic F-84G "Thunderjet"

The F-84G had many firsts which would become distinctive. They became the first to have the new axial-flow turbojet engine combining straight-through airflow making for low-drag characteristics. The first generation fighter for the U.S. replacing the Lockheed F-80C, and supplementing the new North American F-86 "Sabre." It flew the Atlantic Ocean non stop. The F-84G was designed to carry a nuclear warhead missile, and was capable of inflight refueling (E Models). It had an autopilot and was the first aircraft used by the newly created USAF "Thunderbirds" Acrobatic team. The F-84G proved to be a very effective ground support fighter-bomber, serving with NATO and in the Korean conflict. This F-84G was dropped from the USAF inventory in October 1957. HAFB was a specialized repair center for the F-84's until 1958.

Specifications:

Type:	Subsonic Tactical Fighter-bomber
Crew:	1
Wingspan:	36 ft 5 in
Length:	38 ft 1 in
Height:	12 ft 7 in
Weight:	23,525 lb.
Engine:	Allison J35 of 5,600 lb. thrust
Service Ceiling:	40,500 ft
Speed:	622 mph
Cost:	$147,699
Armament:	6 .50 cal. guns, plus 4,000 lb. ordnance

Republic F-84G "Thunderjet" S/N 52-3242

10 Feb. 1953	Delivered to the USAF by Republic Aviation, Long Island, NY
Feb. 1953	To 12th Strategic Fighter Wg. (SAC) Bergstrom AFB, TX
May 1954	To 20th Fighter Bomber Wg. (USAFE) Wethersfield RAF Station, England
Jun. 1954	To Brookley Air Material Area
Mar. 1956	To Dallas,TX for Contract work
Jul. 1956	To 3600th Combat Crew Training WG (ATC) Luke AFB, AZ
Oct. 1956	To 3615th Flying Training WG ATC Craig AFB, AL
Oct. 1956	To 3600th Combat Crew Training Wg. Luke AFB, AZ
Jan. 1957	To 1401st Air Base Wing (MATS), Andrews AFB, DC
Feb. 1957	To 3600th Combat Crew Training Wg. (ATC) Luke AFB, AZ
Jun. 1957	To Ogden AMC
Oct. 1957	Dropped from USAF Inventory

On Display at Midvale City Park for 22 years.

Mar. 1983   Assigned to HAFB Museum for Display

Hill Aerospace Museum has one of only two F-84Gs in the World. No others arc known to still exist.

F-84G prototype set American speed record in 1946 of 611 MPH. It was the first fighter-bomber equipped to carry an atomic bomb. It was also the first fighter-bomber capable of inflight refueling.

North American F-86L "Sabre"

Designed and built in the late 1940s, this fighter first employed the "flying tail" where the entire horizontal stabilizer was rotated to control pitch. In all previous aircraft the horizontal stabilizer were divided into two sections, the front section fixed to the fuselage, and the rear section hinged to the fixed parts. The "flying tail" gives an aircraft much quicker response to control inputs. All jet aircraft designed since then, military as well as commercial, have this feature. It was called a "second generation" jet fighter because its wings were swept back to delay on set of compressibility of air. This D to L model is equipped with a rocket tray for twenty-four "Mighty Mouse" spin stabilized rockets. These were fired shotgun style after the nose radar locked onto the target. HAFB did maintenance and overhaul on the F-86 from 1954 to 1961. The "Sabre" jets were also assigned to the Utah Air National Guard.

Specifications:

Type:	All weather Air Defense Fighter
Crew:	1
Wingspan:	37 ft 1 in
Length:	40 ft 3 in
Height:	15 ft
Weight:	17,806 lb.
Speed:	715 mph
Cost:	$343,839
Service Ceiling:	54,600 ft
Number produced:	2,910
Armament:	24 Mighty Mouse rockets

North American F-86L "Sabre" S/N 51-6055

23 Jul. 1953	Delivered to the USAF North American Aviation, Inglewood, CA
Jul. 1953	To 432nd Fighter Interceptor Sq. (ADC) Truax AFB, WI
Sep. 1954	To 456th Fighter Interceptor Sq. (ADC) Truax AFB, WI
Aug. 1956	To 325th Fighter Interceptor Sq. (ADC) Truax AFB, WI
Sep. 1956	To Sacramento Air Material Area.
Apr. 1957	Modified To F-86L
May 1957	To 3625th Combat Crew Training Wing, Tyndall AFB, FL
Jun. 1957	To 3555th Combat Crew Training Wing, Perrin AFB, TX
Oct. 1961	To 123rd Fighter Interceptor Sq. (ANG), Portland, OR
Nov. 1961	Dropped From USAF Inventory

Was installed on a pedestal in Albany, OR for over 20 years

Jul. 1983	To Hill Aerospace Museum for display

Northrop F-89H "Scorpion"

In the late 1940s the United States felt a need for a jet powered aircraft capable of destroying Soviet-built long range aircraft. The F-89 was designed as an all-weather, night interceptor to replace the Northrop built P-61 "Black Widow." It was built with a powerful radar set housed in the nose. A second crew member operating the radar and could lock on a target in any type of weather, and fire forty-two or forty-eight 70mm. unguided rockets, shotgun style. Later developments included a Genie missile fired from beneath each wing. In its early development, the F-89 had four 20mm. cannons mounted in the nose, and later increased to six. In the D model, rockets replaced the cannon. The Genie missile was added to the J models, and then the Hughes Falcon Missile was added to the J model. The huge permanent wing pods are a combination of rockets tubes in front and fuel in the rear section. The fuel section was is well insulated from rocket blast. The F-89 was phased out in the late 1950s by the F-102 "Delta Dagger." HAFB was Prime Depot for Northrop aircraft parts for the F-89. The F-89 was assigned to HAFB in 1960. This aircraft was dropped from USAF inventory in October of 1960.

Specifications:

Type:	All weather/night fighter interceptor
Crew:	2
Engine:	2 Allison J-35 of 4000 lb. thrust ea.
Cruise:	465 mph
Wingspan:	60 ft
Weight:	47,719 lb.
Length:	53 ft 10 in
Height:	17 ft 6 in
Max. speed:	630 mph
Armament:	48 70mm rockets or two Genie nuclear warheads
Cost:	$1,009,000
Number produced:	1,050

Northrop F-89H "Scorpion" S/N 54-322

29 May 1956   Delivered to the USAF by Northrop Aircraft, Hawthorn, CA
May 1956   To 321st Fighter Interceptor Sq. (ADC) Paine, WA
Jul. 1957   To 326th Consolidated Logistics Maintenance Sq., Paine AFB, WA
Apr. 1958   To 142nd Consolidated Logistics Sq. (ANG) Portland, OR
Oct. 1960   Dropped From USAF inventory
Apr. 1983   To Hill Aerospace Museum for Display

F-89 assembly line at Hill

North American F-100A "Super Sabre"

The F-86 Sabre was so good, it was decided to make a supersonic follow-on, the "Super Sabre." It turned out, however, to be a completely different aircraft in shape and design. It featured 45 degree swept wings, with full span leading edge wing slats, and a large oval-shaped air intake out front, it was designed to take advantage of the tremendous power of the J-57 turbojet engine with afterburner. First flown on 25 May 1953, it was too late for the Korean conflict which prompted its design. The D models had the first autopilot for supersonic aircraft. It proved its sustained supersonic capabilities in level flight by setting a world airspeed record of 822.14 mph in August 1955. It exceeded Mach 1 by more than 62 mph, being the first production aircraft to be able to do so. It was used extensively in Vietnam as a fighter-bomber for close air support operations. The two-seated F model were used as "Wild Weasel" Aircraft for "SAM" suppression. Production halted in 1979. The long tube in front is a pitot tube, which is used to measure airspeed. It was assigned to Hill AFB in 1960.

Specifications:

Type:	Fighter-bomber
Crew:	1
Engine:	Pratt & Whitney J-57, 10,000 - 16,000 lb. thrust
Speed:	cruise 590 mph; max. 864 mph
Wingspan:	38 ft 10 in
Length:	54 ft 2 in
Height:	16 ft 2 in
Weight:	34,832 lb.
Service ceiling:	50,000 ft
Armament:	4 20mm cannon + 7,000 lb. variable ordinance
Cost:	$704,000

North American F-100A "Super Sabre" S/N 52-5777

5 Aug. 1954	Delivered to the USAF by North American Aviation, Inglewood, CA
Aug. 1954	To Air Force Armament Center, Eglin AFB, FL
Dec. 1955	Modified to JF-100A
May 1957	To 3595th Combat Crew Training Wing, (ATC) Nellis AFB, NV
Jun. 1957	Modified to F-100A
May 1958	To 152nd Fighter Interceptor Sq. (ANG), Tucson, AZ
Jun. 1958	To 162nd Consolidated Logistic Maintenance Sq., Tucson, AZ
Apr. 1961	Returned to 152nd at Tucson, AZ
Jan. 1963	To 162nd Fighter Grp. (ANG), Tucson, AZ
May 1966	To Ogden AMC and dropped from USAF inventory

F-100F with canopy open

McDonnell F-101B "Voodoo"

Picture this type of aircraft with an elongated shovel-shaped nose filled with cameras photographing missile sites in Cuba in 1962. An F-101B flew so low it almost hit the ball of Soviet technicians playing volleyball in their off hours. Along with the famous U-2 this type of aircraft brought back the photos of missiles being placed in Cuba that were the basis for a major international confrontation. Fortunately, the Soviets backed off and shipped their missiles home. Designed as a high speed, high altitude, long range penetration fighter-interceptor. It became the heaviest and fastest yet to enter the USAF inventory. Setting an airspeed record of 1,207 mph, it was built to be an escort for the B-36 until that huge aircraft was replaced by the B-52. The C model could carry 6,720 lb. of bombs, including a nuclear weapons. Early models had four 20mm cannons, mounted under the nose. The RF-101C was used in Vietnam for reconnaissance missions being our first supersonic photo-recon aircraft. It was used by the Royal Canadian Air Force until the mid-1970s. A few were acquired by the Chinese Nationalist Air Force. Production ended in March 1961. Nuclear weapons could be carried between the drop tanks on the fuselage. The sensor in front of the pilot's windscreen locked the radar-directed rockets on an enemy target. This type aircraft was assigned to HAFB in 1960s.

Specifications:

Type:	Long-range all-weather interceptor
Crew:	2
Wingspan:	39 ft 8 in
Length:	67 ft 4 in
Height:	18 ft
Weight:	52,400 lb.
Engines:	2 Pratt & Whitney J-57, 16,900 lb. thrust each
Speed:	1,220 mph.
Cost:	$1,819,000

McDonnell F-101B "Voodoo" S/N 57-252

10 May 1959	Delivered to the USAF by McDonnell Aircraft, St. Louis, MO
May 1959	To 78th Fighter Group (ADC) Hamilton AFB, CA
Sep. 1960	To 478th Fighter Group (ADC) Grand Forks AFB, ND
Feb. 1961	To 478th Fighter Wing (ADC) Grand Forks AFB, ND
Dec. 1961	Returned to 78th Fighter Group Hamilton AFB, CA
Jul. 1968	To 445th Interceptor Sq. (ADC), Wurtsmith AFB, MI
Sep. 1968	To 75th Fighter Interceptor Sq. (ADC),Wurtsmith, MI
Nov. 1969	To 119th Fighter Group (ANG), Hector, ND
Aug. 1978	To San Antonio AMA
Oct. 1978	To 147th Fighter Interceptor Group (ANG), Ellington AFB, TX
Jun. 1982	Dropped from USAF Inventory

F-101s on assembly line at Hill

Convair F-102A "Delta Dagger"

Built first as the XF-92, it could not meet its design specifications for supersonic speed. The problem? Transonic drag exceeded engine power. Translation: air flow around the fuselage conflicted with airflow over the wings producing turbulence and a vacuum, slowing the aircraft drastically. The solution: slim out the fuselage and pinch it to a coke bottle shape. Now, if you look at the fuselage where the numbers FC-833 appear, you will see how they radically reworked the fuselage. The aircraft met its design specifications on the next flight. You can also see this pinched-waist feature on the B-1B and the F-16, both supersonic aircraft. It replaced the F-89 "Scorpion" in the USAF's coastal and border defense roles. From the 1950s to the 1970s many a Soviet Aircrew flying near the coast of the U.S. have seen these aircraft on their wing. It has a highly sophisticated MG-3 fire control system capability and its safety record in Vietnam was a loss of only 15 in seven years of escort work for the B-52s. It was used by the USAF until 1974 and withdrawn from service in 1978. Ogden was the specialized repair activity for this aircraft and did maintenance and modification for Iran from 1957 to 1962. Later it was used by Greece and Turkey. The long tube on the front of the fuselage is a pitot tube, the pilot's airspeed sensor.

Specifications:

Type:	Supersonic all-weather interceptor
Crew:	1
Engine:	1 P&W J-57 of 16,000 lb. thrust w/afterburner
Cruise:	600 mph
Wingspan:	38 ft 1 in
Length:	68 ft 4 in
Height:	21 ft 4 in
Weight:	31,559 lb.
Cost:	$1,184,000
Armament:	24 unguided FFAR rockets, 6 guided Hughes A1M-4A and AIM-4C missiles

Convair F-102A "Delta Dagger" S/N 57-833

4 Jun. 1958	Delivered to the USAF by Convair Division of General Dynamics, San Diego, CA
Jun. 1958	To 329th Fighter Interceptor Squadron (ADC) George AFB, CA
May 1960	To 82nd Fighter Interceptor Sq. (ADC), Travis AFB, CA
Dec. 1965	To 337th Fighter Gp (ADC) Portland, OR
Jan. 1966	To 142nd Fighter Gp (ANG), Portland, OR
Jun. 1970	Dropped from the USAF Inventory
Apr. 1983	To HAFB for display at Museum

Roaring high over the Mojave Desert in Southern California, Convair's delta-wing interceptor, the F102A, creates a deceptive picture of floating in the clouds. Magnitude of the big, all-weather Air Force plane is easily seen by comparing it with the pilot in the white helmet. The size of a World War II medium bomber, Convair's F-102A locks on and fires by radar.

Republic F-105D "Thunderchief"

Revered for its toughness and durability it was affectionately known as the "Thud." The F-105s aircraft carried out 75% of the bomb strike missions in Vietnam. Described as the workhorse of Vietnam, it became known for its ability to penetrate enemy defense forces at supersonic speeds, make the strike, and streak home to fight another day. It was the largest and heaviest fighter bomber in the USAF inventory and was four years in planning. It was designed as an all-weather supersonic strike fighter-bomber. The F-105 was designed to carry four tons of bombs, including nuclear weapons. It is unique in that it has an internal fuselage bomb bay. It carried only conventional bombs in Vietnam, four tons internally and three tons externally. The six barrels of the Vulcan cannon are capable of pouring out 100 rds of 20 mm ammunition per second. The eight Nazi Swastikas are the credits for Nazi aircraft downed by Col. Paul P. Douglas in a P-47 in WWII and were painted on this aircraft which he flew when he served in Vietnam in the mid-60s. He was also known as the "Arkansas Traveler." HAFB had prime supply and maintenance responsibilities for the F-105 beginning in 1954.

Specifications:

Type:	Long range all-weather fighter-bomber
Crew:	1
Service ceiling:	52,000 ft
Engine:	1 Pratt & Whitney J-75
Range:	1,840 miles
Cruise:	600 mph; max. speed 1,480 mph
Wingspan:	34 ft 2 in
Height:	20 ft 2 in
Length:	69 ft 1 in
Armament:	M-61 Vulcan 20mm cannon + 4 x AIM-9s +7 tons ordnance
Cost:	$5,649,543
Total produced:	833

Republic F-105D "Thunderchief" S/N 59-1743

Nov. 1960	Delivered to USAF by Republic Aviation, Farmington, NY
Dec. 1960	To 4520th Combat Crew Training Wg. (TAC), Nellis AFB, NV
Apr. 1964	To 4th Tactical Fighter Wg. (TAC), Seymour Johnson AFB, NC
Jun. 1966	To 388th Tactical Fighter Wing (PACAF), Korat RTAB, Thailand
May 1969	To 355th Fighter Wg. (PACAF), Tahkli RTAB, Thailand
Oct. 1970	To 23rd Tactical Fighter Wg. (TAC), McConnell AFB, KS
Jan. 1971	To 192nd Tactical Fighter Wg. (TAC), Byrd Field, TX
Feb. 1981	Dropped from the USAF inventory

Last F-105D MiG killer in service at HAFB

Last F-105D Thud unit in service at HAFB

Republic F-105G "Thunderchief"

("Wild Weasel")

This aircraft has the sharp teeth and mouth painted on it and is a later version of the F-105D. The long conspicuous tubes along the lower fuselage on both sides contained electronic equipment used for "Wild Weasel" operations. Wild Weasel operations involved the location and destruction of SAMS (Surface-to-Air Missiles Sites). This additional mission for the F-105 further proved its versatility and usefulness as a strike weapons system. This aircraft had a crew of two: the pilot and an Electronics Warfare Officer. The crews of this aircraft claimed three MIG kills. This aircraft was assigned to the 388th TFW at Korat RTAB, Thailand in November 1972. HAFB had prime supply, maintenance, and specialized depot responsibilities for the F-105 starting in 1954. The 419th TFW flew this type aircraft at Hill AFB.

Specifications:

Type:	Long range all-weather fighter-bomber
Crew:	2
Power Plant:	1 Pratt & Whitney J-75, 26,500 lb. thrust w/ab.
Wingspan:	34 ft 11 in
Length:	69 ft 1 in
Height:	20 ft 2 in
Weight:	54,000 lb.
Speed:	1,480 mph
Cost:	$5,649,543
Armament:	M-61 Vulcan 20mm cannon + 4 Shrikes + 7 tons ordnance

Republic F-105G "Thunderchief" S/N 62-440 WW ("Wild Weasel")

Feb. 19, 1964	Delivered to USAF by Republic Aviation, Farmingdale, NY
Mar. 1964	To 4th TFW (TAC) Seymour Johnson AFB, NC
Nov. 1964	To Incirlik, Turkey
May 1965	To Seymour Johnson AFB, NC
Sep. 1965	To 4520th CCTW (TAC) Nellis AFB, NV
Nov. 1967	To 23rd TFW (TAC) McConnell AFB, KS
Aug. 1972	To 561st TFW (TAC) McConnell AFB, KS
Oct. 1972	To 15th ABW (PACAF) Hickam AFB, HI
Nov. 1972	To 288th TFW (TACAF) Korat RTAB, Thailand
Oct. 1974	To 35th TFW (TAC) George AFB, CA
Oct. 1979	To 116th TFW (ANG) Dobbins AFB, GA
Dec. 1982	To Hill Aerospace Museum for Display

General Dynamics F-111E "Aardvark"

In November 1962 General Dynamics was awarded a contract to develop the "Swing Wing" TFX as a joint Air Force and Navy Fighter. The differing requirements were difficult to reconcile, and the F111B Naval model was canceled. The A model first flew in December 1964, and entered service in October 1967. Early aircraft were deployed to the Vietnam War in March 1968 and the loss of two out of six aircraft in five days proved that development was incomplete. The aircraft was taken out of service until further research could be done. Many changes were developed and the aircraft was used in the retaliatory attack on Libya in 1986. The F model was used in 1991 in the Persian Gulf War. The aircraft was primarily used in night raids during Desert Storm. It flew day time missions using GBU-15 Guided Bomb Units to seal the oil pipeline manifold that was allowing oil to flow into the Persian Gulf. This F-111 comes to the Museum from RAF Station Upper Heyford, England. This particular aircraft was flown by OOALC Commander Lt/Gen. Dale Thompson and former Base Commander Col. Steve Emery who was an EWO. The aircraft last flew 7-8 December 1993.

Specifications:

Type:	Two-seat all-weather attack & strike aircraft
Engines:	2 25,000 lb. thrust Pratt & Whitney TF30-P-100 turbofans
Speed:	1,650 mph at 36,000 ft
Service Ceiling:	60,000 ft
Range:	2,925+ miles
Wingspan:	63 ft fully spread & 31 ft 11 in full sweep
Length:	73 ft 6 in
Height:	17 ft 1.5 in
Weight:	Empty 47,481 lb.; take-off 100,000 lb.
Armament:	1 20-mm multi-barrel cannon with up to 31,500 lb. of ordnance
Cost:	$18 million
Total produced:	225

General Dynamics F-111E "Aardvark" S/N 68-020

Principal Versions

F-111 Early aircraft with TF30-P-3 engines	159
F-111B Naval models discontinued due cost and overweight	0
F-111C Australian aircraft combining the F-111A with the wings of the FB-111A Strategic Bomber models.	24
F-111D aircraft with better electronic and the TP30-P-9 engine	96
F-111E aircraft with improved engine inlets and an inertial navigation system.	94
F-111F aircraft of the definitive model with all-round improvement of airframe and electronics, and upgraded in service with advanced targeting equipment.	94
Total Produced	467

Item of Interest:

Note found in the cockpit after this aircraft was received at the Museum:

"This aircraft, F-111E 68-020, 20th Fighter Wing's 'Chief' last flown
7 & 8 Dec. 1993 from RAF Upper Heyford, UK to Hill AFB, UT, via Wright-Patterson AFB,
OH, by Col. Mark Schmidt, 20th FW Commander and Lt. Col. Daniel C. Clark, 20th FW
Operations Group Commander."

Model of the F-111E showing the way the "swing wing" works

McDonnell-Douglas F-15 "Eagle"

The F-15 was designed as a twin engine aircraft with advanced avionics including a fly-by-wire control system and the APG-63 radar. Later models used the APG-70 radar. During trials it displayed phenomenal performance. It entered service in January 1976. Later modifications included up-dated electronics and provisions for FAST (Fuel And Sensor Tactical) packs. These packs are attached in the angle between the engine trunks and the under surfaces of the wings, providing greater fuel capacity. These packs also provide additional weapon attachment points without any significant drag problems. There have been five F-15 models: The F-15A initial single-seated model; The F-15B a two-seated model; The F-15C improved single-seated model with more capable electronic counter measures and provisions for the new AIM-120 AMRAAM air-to-air missiles; The F-15D An improved two-seated model; The F-15E Eagle the world's finest air superiority and all-weather attack aircraft.

Specifications:

Type:	air superiority/attack fighter
Engines:	2 Pratt & Whitney F-100-P-100, 23,950 lb. thrust
Performance:	Max. 1,650 mph
Service ceiling:	60,000 ft
Range:	2,878 miles
Weight:	empty 27,000 lb.
Wingspan:	42 ft 9.75 in
Length:	63 ft 9 in
Height:	18 ft 5.5 in
Armament:	1 20-mm multi-barrel cannon and up to 23,600 lb. of disposable stores
Cost:	N/A

McDonnell-Douglas F-15 "Eagle" S/N 77-090

Oct. 1978	Delivered to USAF by McDonnell-Douglas, St. Louis, MO
Nov. 1978	To 32nd Tactical Fighter Sq. (US Air Forces Europe), Camp New Amsterdam, Netherlands
Jul. 1980	To 33rd Tactical Fighter Wing (TAC), Eglin AFB, FL
Nov. 1982	To 57th Fighter Weapons Wing (TAC), Nellis AFB, NV
Feb. 1984	To 405th Tactical Fighter Wing (TAC), Luke AFB, AZ
Feb. 1992	To 325th Fighter Wing (TAC), Tyndall AFB, FL
Mar. 1994	To HAFB Museum for display

F-15 on the ramp with ground crewmen

General Dynamics F-16A "Fighting Falcon"

During 1971, the USAF asked five companies to develop concepts for a highly maneuverable, light-weight fighter using advanced aerodynamics and a "fly-by-wire" control system. Prototype contracts were awarded to General Dynamics (YF-16) and Northrop (YF-17). In January 1975 the YF-16 was declared winner of the Light-Weight Fighter competition. The USAF program produced 3,250 aircraft. In addition to US production there is a European construction consortium that will produce the F-16 for European consumption. The F-16 is on the cutting edge of technology especially in the later versions that included sophisticated avionics sensors for low-level navigation and night attack. These later models are the F-16C and F-16D which possess, in addition to better electronics and more modern weapons for multi-role use, the capability to accommodate either of two engine types. The F-16 was assigned to Hill AFB, Utah in the early 1980s and are flown by both the 388th and 419th TFWs. The aircraft at the Museum is an A model and formerly assigned to the 388th TFW.

Specifications:

Type:	air superiority/ground attack fighter
Engine:	1 General Electric F110-GE-100 or Pratt & Whitney F100-P-220 turbofan, with 27,600 lb. of thrust
Speed:	Max. 1,320+ mph
Range:	575+ miles
Weights:	empty 18,335 lb.
Wingspan:	32 ft 9.75 in
Length:	49 ft 4 in
Height:	16 ft 8.5 in
Armament:	1 20-mm multi-barrel cannon + up to 20,450 lb. Ordnance
Cost:	N/A

General Dynamics F-16A "Fighting Falcon" S/N 78-065

Mar. 1980	Delivered to USAF by General Dynamics, Fort Worth, TX
Mar. 1980	To 388th Tactical Fighter Sq. (TAC) Hill AFB, UT
Oct. 1980	To Hill AFB, UT
Apr. 1982	To 56th Tactical Training Wing (TAC) MacDill AFB, FL
Feb. 1984	To 466th Tactical Fighter Sq. (USAFR) Hill AFB, UT
Feb. 1994	To Hill Aerospace Museum

Flight test F-16 on runway at HAFB

McDonnell-Douglas F/A-18 "Hornet"

Northrop teamed with McDonnell-Douglas to produce a significantly revised single-seat fighter. This was for an aircraft designed to meet ambitious naval requirements. This requirement was for a single aircraft to replace the McDonnell Douglas F-4 and Vought A-7 in the multi-role fighter and attack roles. The F-18 first flew in November 1978. It's size, configuration, and advanced electronics provided capability in both roles merely by software alterations. With McDonnell Douglas as prime contractor, deliveries began in 1980. Total deliveries for the US Navy and Marine Corps are 410 aircraft.

Specifications:

Type:	single-seat carrier and land based fighter and attack
Engines:	2 16,000-lb. thrust F404-GE-400 turbofans
Wingspan:	400.0 sq. ft
Length:	56 ft
Height:	15 ft 3.5 in
Weight:	49,224 lb.
Speed:	1,188+ mph
Number produced:	410
Armament:	1 20-mm multi-barrel cannon + up to 17,000 lb. Ordnance

McDonnell-Douglas F/A-18 "Hornet" S/N 161725

Last station: Naval Air Station, Joint Reserve Base, New Orleans, LA
                                transferred to USAF from USN

Feb. 96   To Hill AFB Museum for display

Lockheed SR-71C "Blackbird"

The SR-71's unique capabilities as a strategic reconnaissance aircraft have given volumes of information to the USAF, US Navy, CIA, and the Defense Intelligence Agency. It collected information during Vietnam, the 1973 Yom Kippur War, Lebanon, Libya, the Falkland Islands, and the Persian Gulf War. Its advantage over satellite observation is that it can be assigned to an arbitrary route, rerun, or crossrun. A satellite observation is limited to a preplanned one-time pass over the target area. SR-71 pilots have pointed out at least eighty arbitrary re-runs all made to back up satellite observations. We should mention its ability to outrun missiles over Vietnam. No SR-71 ever suffered a missile hit from the 1,000 or so missiles reported by pilots who have been fired upon.

The SR-71's history began on 21 April 1958 when Kelly Johnson proposed an A-1 through A-12 (A-meaning attack) designs to the CIA and the USAF. The CIA gave initial approval to construction of three in September 1959 and the aircraft made its first flight 31 months later. The first flight was flown by Louis W. Schalk. The A-12 was intended as a follow-on reconnaissance aircraft to the replace the U-2, which had become vulnerable to SAMs. Three A-12s were later converted to SR-71s. More SR-71s were ordered by the USAF in late December 1962. All Blackbird versions have the same wingspan, but the SR-71 is a longer, heavier and more improved design. It is not maneuverable at high speeds, and it is costly to operate: $18,000 per hour. For a normal run of twelve hours the cost was $216,000. One year's operation, would cost $200 to $300 million. The SR-71 can photograph topography at the rate of 35 miles every minute and survey an area of 60,000 square miles in one hour. On 26 April 1971 an SR-71 completed a 15,000 mile non-stop flight around the U.S. using inflight refueling.

Our hybrid aircraft consists of the rear section of S/N 1001/60-06934 (the first YF-12A) and an engineering mockup forward fuselage. This was the only SR-71C ever built and was used for pilot training. This aircraft is always referred to as the "Bastard," and had a total of 555.4 flight hours.

Specifications:

Type:	Strategic electronic and photo reconnaissance
Crew:	2
Engines:	2 Pratt & Whitney J-58 turbojets, 32,500 lb. thrust ea.
Wingspan:	55 ft 7 in
Length:	107 ft 5 in
Weight:	127,000 lb.
Speed:	2,432 mph at 79,000 ft
Number produced:	49
Armament:	None
Cost:	Estimated at $25 million (1959 dollars)

Lockheed SR-71C "Blackbird" S/N 64-17981

Program approved 29 Aug. 1959 - 31 months to test flight

7 Aug. 1963	Maiden flight of the prototype YF-12 first flown by Col. Robert L. Stephens and Lt. Col. Daniel Andre. S/N 60-6934 (1001)
1 May 1965	An attempt was made to establish a new speed record. The flight was aborted because of engine malfunctions and the aircraft was involved in a runway accident. It had 180.9 flight hours. It was later converted to the SR-71C.
24 Jun. 1967	The FY-12 is processed for extended storage.
14 Mar. 1969	The SR-71C S/N 2000/64-17981 made its maiden flight from Palmdale SR-71 Flight Test Facility, Site 2.
3 Sep. 1970	Aircraft delivered to Beale AFB, CA
20 Oct. 1976	Removed from storage.
25 Aug. 1990	SR-71C Arrived at Hill Aerospace Museum for display.

A total of 49 aircraft (17 YA-12s and 32 SR-71s) were produced. Our aircraft was number 49.

SR-71 Aircraft today:

Warner-Robbins AFB

Castle Air Museum

Smithsonian Museum

Wright-Patterson AFB

Hill Aerospace Museum

Edwards AFB

Seattle Museum of Flight

NY Sea-Air Space Museum

Alabama Space & Rocket Center

March AFB

Lackland AFB

Offutt AFB

Beale AFB

Pima Air Museum

Chicago Museum of Science

Minnesota ANG Museum

San Diego Aerospace Museum

Seven are also held at Palmdale and Edwards AFBs

NOTE: On 25 December 95, 3 SR-71s were returned to service for use at NASA at the cost of $100 million. These aircraft will be flying from Beale AFB, California for space exploration. (From Capt. Michael Zimmerman, Restoration Manager, Wright-Patterson AFB)

Lockheed T-33A "Thunderbird"

Affectionately known as the "T-Bird" by thousands of pilots who trained in this aircraft, it was the training version of the F-80C "Shooting Star," America's first pure jet fighter. To accommodate the student-in-training, the fuselage of the F-80C was lengthened 38.5 inches—the canopy was also lengthened. This changed the aerodynamics of the aircraft so that the two-seated T-33 was faster than the single-seated F-80C. Aerodynamically the F-80C is an exceptionally clean aircraft. Beginning in March 1948, for more than twenty years it was used to train more pilots for jet flight than any other trainer. Our aircraft was used by the 461st Bombardment Group in the late 1950s and assigned to Hill AFB in 1960.

Specifications:

Type:	Trainer
Crew:	2
Engine:	1 Allison J-33 Turbojet at 6100 lb. thrust
Cruise:	440 mph
Wingspan:	38 ft 10 in
Length:	37 ft 10 in
Weight:	14,000 lb.
Height:	11 ft 4 in
Armament:	6 .50 cal. Browning machine guns on some models
Cost:	Not given
Total Produced:	5,691

Lockheed T-33A "Thunderbird" S/N 51-9271

18 Jun. 1953	Delivered to the USAF by Lockheed Aircraft, Burbank, CA
Jun. 1953	To 3580th Pilot Training Wing (ATC), Foster AFB, TX
Jun. 1954	To 3505th Pilot Training Wing (ATC), Greenville AFB, MS
Aug. 1960	To 3560th Pilot Training Wing (ATC), Webb AFB, TX
Jul. 1961	To 32nd Fighter Wing (ADC), MONOT AFB, ND
Jun. 1962	To 5th Fighter Interceptor Sq. (ADC), Monot AFB, ND
Apr. 1966	To Ogden Air Material Area
May 1966	Dropped From USAF Inventory

T-33 in Tripoli in 1956

Cessna T-37 "Tweet"

The Cessna T-37 (A-37 Dragonfly) was originally built as a trainer for the USAF. It was modified for use in Southeast Asia as a close air support aircraft. It was popular as a light strike aircraft because of its slow speed which allowed it to bomb accurately and operate in weather conditions unfavorable to other high speed aircraft. It had six wing stations that could be armed with MK-82 bombs and BLU-3-B Napalm tanks. It could carry a wide assortment of machine guns, rockets, flares, and bombs. This aircraft is not pressurized and is not fitted with an ejection seat. The crew is protected by layered nylon flak curtains. Because of its simplicity, maintenance was easy to perform. This type aircraft was widely used as a trainer.

Specifications:

Type:	Dual-seat trainer
Crew:	2 (Instructor & Student Pilot)
Wingspan:	35 ft 10.5 in
Height:	29 ft 3 in
Weight:	loaded 14,000 lb.
Speed:	507 mph
Range:	1,012 miles
Armament:	T-37 none; A-37 wide variety of armaments and ordnance
Cost:	N/A

Cessna T-37 "Tweet" S/N 57-2259

Aug. 1958	Delivered to USAF by Cessna Aircraft Corp, Wichita, KS
Aug. 1958	To 3303rd Pilot Training (Contract) Gp (ATC) Bartow AFB, FL
Jan. 1961	To 3525th Pilot Training Wing (ATC) Williams AFB, AZ (to T-37B)
Jan. 1973	To 82nd Flying Training Wing (ATC) Williams AFB, AZ
Jan. 1974	To 88th Flying Training Sq. (ATC) Sheppard AFB, TX
Sep. 1976	To 64th Flying Training Wing (ATC) Reese AFB, TX
Nov. 1991	To USAF Museum Program as display aircraft
Aug. 1992	To HAFB Museum

Northrop T-38A "Talon"

The Talon was the first supersonic aircraft designed for the specific role as a trainer. It was designed to replace the T-33. The first Talons were powered by two non-afterburner type engines. Each YJ85-GE-1 turbojet was rated at 2,100 lb. of thrust. It was first flown on 10 April 1959. The first production model was flown in January 1960. Current models use the J-85GE-5 engines. The Talon entered service with the USAF with the Air Training Command at Randolph AFB in March 1961. The first order was for sixty-nine aircraft and later increased to 213. Hill AFB had prime responsibility for the T-38.

Specifications:

Type:	Two-seat Trainer
Speed:	818 mph
Power Plant:	2 J-85-GE- 5 turbojets
Weight:	11,650 lb.
Wing Span:	25 ft 3 in
Length:	44 ft 2 in
Height:	12 ft 10 in
Cost:	N/A

Northrop T-38A "Talon" S/N 61-0824

Feb. 1962	Delivered to USAF by Northrop Aircraft Corp. Hawthorne, CA
Jul. 1962	To 3560th Pilot Training Wing (ATC) Webb AFB, TX
Nov. 1972	To San Antonio Air Logistics Area, Kelly AFB, TX
Dec. 1975	To AF Logistics Command, Pintaung North AP, Taiwan
Nov. 1976	To Military Aircraft Storage and Disposition Center, Davis-Monthan AFB, AZ
Jul. 1978:	To Sheppard Technical Training Center (ATC) Sheppard AFB, TX (to GT-38A, ground instruction airframe)
Mar. 1992	To HAFB Museum

North American T-39 "Sabreliner"

The Sabreliner made its maiden flight on 16 September 1958 as the newest member of the Sabre family of high-performance aircraft. North American went ahead with the NA-246 as a private venture to meet the USAF's requirement for a utility aircraft and combat readiness trainer. Besides having the capability for the training of multi-engine pilots, navigators, and instrument rating instructors the T-39 has the facility for passenger or cargo carrying. The aircraft may be flown from either cockpit seat. Features include 20 degree swept wings, tricycle landing gear, nose gear power steering, speed brakes, and aerodynamically operated wing slats. It can be serviced from the ground. Internal batteries provide a self-starting capability. The air conditioning system provides a complete change of air every two minutes. The pressurization system generates an 8,000 cabin pressure at 45,000 feet.

Specifications:

Type:	Utility jet trainer and transport
Crew:	2
Power Plant:	2 Pratt & Whitney J-60 Single Shaft
Wingspan:	44 ft 5 in
Length:	43 ft 9 in
Height:	16 ft
Weight:	17,760 lb.
Speed:	595 mph at 21,500 ft; cruise 500 mph at 43,600 ft
Range:	1,430 miles
Cost:	N/A
Armament:	None

North American Aviation T-39 "Sabreliner" S/N 61-0674

Sep. 1962	Delivered to USAF by North American Aviation, Inglewood, CA
Oct. 1962	To 3rd Bombardment (TAC) Wing (Pacific Air Forces) Yokota AB, Japan
Jun. 1965	To 41st Air Division Hdqrs. (PACAF) Yokota AB, Japan
Jan. 1968	To 347th Tactical Fighter Wing (PACAF) Yokota AB, Japan
Jan. 1969	To 475th Tactical Fighter Wing (PACAF) Misawa AB, Japan
Nov. 1969	To 63rd Military Airlift Wing (MATS) Norton AFB, CA
Apr. 1975	To 1400th Military Airlift Sq. (MAC) Norton AFB, CA
Jun. 1977	To CT-39A
Jun. 1985	Dropped from inventory by transfer to school or museum
Sep. 1993	To Hill AFB Museum from Norton AFB Museum

LTV YA-7F "Corsair II"

Only two of these F models were built by LTV Corporation. The first YA-7F prototype made its maiden flight on 29 November 1989 from the LTV Dallas facility. The second prototype flew on 3 April 1990. Both YA-7Fs underwent a flight test program at LTV Dallas and were then flown to Edwards AFB, California for U.S. Air Force tests. The flight test program was conducted by the 6510th Test Wing. The test program was terminated in late 1990 after the Air Force made its decision to purchase a ground attack version of the General Dynamics F-16 Fighting Falcon. The other YA-7F is at Edwards AFB and will be placed on display in non-flyable condition at the Edwards Museum. The A7 was used in Vietnam as a FAC (Forward Air Controller) aircraft. It was used to drop chaff for the F-4 Wild Weasels at the end of the Vietnam War. A-7s were used in the SS Mayaguez incident in May 1975 off Koh Tang Island as a FAC to draw enemy fire. We are very lucky to have the second YA-7F in our museum.

Specifications:

Type:	Fighter-Bomber
Weight:	42,000 lb. gross
Engines:	1 Allison TF-41-A-2 Turbofan 15,000 lb. thrust
Crew:	1
Length:	46 ft 1 1/2 in
Wing Span:	38 ft 9 in
Height:	16 ft 3/4 in
Speed:	max. 690 mph; cruise 470 mph
Armament:	Misc. bombs, Paveway Laser-Guided bombs
Cost:	N/A

LTV YA-7F "Corsair II" S/N 71-1039

Manufacturer	LTV, Dallas, TX
Apr. 1992	To Hill AFB Museum for display from Dallas, TX

Mikoyan-Guryevich MiG-21F "Fishbed C"

In the autumn of 1953, the Soviet experimental-design bureau headed by Colonel-General Artem Ivanovich Mikoyan and mathematician Mikhaillosifovich Guryevich began work to meet the official requirement for a new short-range fighter interceptor. Their prototype, known as the Ye-2, was unveiled in early 1955 and the Ye-6 variant was first seen in public at the Soviet Aviation Day at Tuchino Airport, Moscow on June 24, 1956. Subsequently known as the MiG-21, this design, and others from the MIG OKB (Opytno Konstruktorskoe Byuro), is acknowledged as the most widely exported fighter "family" in the world. This MiG-21F-13 is a short-range, clear weather fighter equipped with an SRD-5 (High-Fix) radar rangefinder inside the movable intake shock cone. Its weapons consist of one internally mounted NR-30 (Nudelman-Rikter 30mm) cannon with a rate of fire of 85 rounds/minute on the starboard side. Externally there are two underwing pylons for carrying rocket pods, small bombs, air-to-ground rockets, or air-to-air missiles. The primary air-to-air missile is the Russian K-13, also known as the AA-2 ATOLL. The ATOLL is a short range, fire and forget, passive infra-red (IR) homing intercept missile. It is patterned after the American AIM-9B Sidewinder. This aircraft has a normal combat radius of 375 miles. Its Tumansky RD-11 afterburning engine provides a maximum of 12,500 lb. thrust. With an average take-off weight of 16,000 pounds it has thrust-to-weight ratio of .78. There are still nearly 5,000 MiG-21s of all types. (Fishbed C through R Series are in use by at least 38 air forces around the world.)

Specifications:

Manufacturer:	State Industries, 1957
Engine:	Turmansky R-11, Turbojet, 12.676 lb. thrust
Wingspan:	23 ft 6 in
Length:	44 ft 2 in
Height:	14 ft 9 in
Weight:	16,700 lb. loaded
Max. Speed:	1,243 mph
Ceiling:	65.610 ft
Range:	350 miles
Armament:	1 x 30mm Cannon, 2 x K-13 Missiles
Crew:	1
Cost:	N/A

Sikorsky CH-3 "Jolly Green Giant"

The CH-3 has been extensively up-rated since the introduction of the initial A model. In 1966, the USAF ordered a more powerful version of the CH-3 and it became the HH-53B. They flew long range search and rescue missions during the Vietnam War and came to be called the "Super Jolly Green Giant." The 1550th ATTW was assigned to Hill AFB and began training in the HH-3 on 1 April 1971. The school graduated about 1,200 pilots and aircrew members annually for USAF and foreign countries in this and other types of choppers. The unit was active at Hill AFB Utah until 15 March 1976 when it transferred to Kirtland AFB New Mexico.

Specifications:

Engine:	2 General Electric T-58-5 turboshafts 1500 hp each
Main rotor diameter:	62 ft
Fuselage Length:	73 ft
Width:	15 ft. 3 in.
Height:	18 ft 1 in.
Weight:	Take Off 22,050
Range :	465 miles
Speed:	465 mph Cruising: 162 mph
Date of Service:	1966
Cost:	N/A

Sikorsky CH-3 "Jolly Green Giant" S/N 65-12790

Aug. 1966	Delivered to USAF by Sikorsky Aircraft, Bridgeport, CT
Dec. 1966	To 100th Strategic Wing (Strategic Air Command) Davis-Monthan AFB, AZ
Feb. 1968	To DaNang AB, Vietnam
Jul. 1969	To Sikorsky Aviation, Bridgeport, CT
Dec. 1969	To 100th Strategic Wing (SAC) Davis-Monthan AFB, AZ
Dec. 1970	To DaNang AB, Vietnam
Nov. 1972	To Nakhon Phanom RTAFB, Thailand
Jul. 1975	To 100th Strategic Reconnaissance Wing (SAC) Davis-Monthan AFB, AZ
Jul. 1976	To 432nd Tactical Drone Group (TAC) Davis-Monthan AFB, AZ
Nov. 1976	To 6514th Test Squadron (AF Systems Command) Hill AFB, UT

Bell TH-13T "Sioux"

The M*A*S*H helicopter! There is probably not an American child or adult who has not seen this bird on TV bringing casualties into the 4077th MASH unit. Spiced with humor and philosophy MASH exposes the realities of war. It was during the Korean War that the capabilities of the helicopter were best demonstrated, including this aircraft. It could carry one or two troops or two stretcher cases outside the cabin. Casualty evacuation by helicopter was more direct and much faster, saving thousands of lives. Later models of helicopters carried the casualties inside. This model first flew on 8 December 1945. It was used by the USAF as well as twenty-seven other nations. Very durable, some variations of this aircraft can still be seen in the air today. This aircraft was used by the Utah Army National Guard.

Specifications:

Type:	Light casualty evacuation helicopter
Crew:	1
Engine:	1 Lycoming TVO=435 piston, 240 hp.
Rotor span:	37 ft 2 in
Length:	31 ft 7 in
Height:	9 ft 3 in
Weight:	1,794 lb.
Speed:	105 mph
Cost:	N/A
Armament:	None
Range:	238 miles

Bell TH-13T "Sioux" S/N 3760

Manufacturer	Bell Aircraft Corp.
Sep. 1987	To Hill Aerospace Museum from Tennessee Valley Authority, Muscle Shoals, AL

Piasecki H-21B "Workhorse"

A nd a workhorse it was! Nicknamed the "Flying Banana" because of the shape of its fuselage, it was also called "Shawnee" by the U.S. Army. The first tandem rotor helicopter to be used by the armed services, it solved the problem of torque, which is present in single rotor helicopters, because one rotor canceled the torque effect of the other. It was used to transport personnel, equipment, and cargo; for rescue; as an assault transport; and for casualty evacuation on an underslung hook. It could carry 4,000 pounds of cargo. Internally it could carry the equivalent weight in personnel and equipment such as 20 fully equipped troops or 11 litter patients. It was used by the USAF in the Arctic because it could operate in temperatures down to 65 degrees below. With additional fuel tanks it made a non-stop distance record of 1,199 miles. It flew non-stop from San Diego, California to Washington D.C. being refueled four times in flight. Designed by Piasecki, it first flew 11 April 1952. It has been used by the USAF, the U.S. Army, French Navy, Royal Canadian Air Force, and West Germany. It was assigned to HAFB in July 1962.

Specifications:

Type:	General purpose transport
Crew:	2
Engine:	1 Wright cyclone R-1820 425 hp
Rotor Span:	44 ft
Length:	52 ft 7 in
Height:	15 ft 4 in
Weight:	10,233 lb.
Cruise:	90 mph
Cost:	$406,000
Armament:	None

Piasecki H-21B "Workhorse" S/N 54-4002

Aug. 1957	Delivered to USAF by Nertol at Morton, PA
Aug. 1957	To 20th Helicopter Sq. (Tactical Air Command) Stewart AFB, TN
Jul. 1959	To Myrtle Beach AFB, SC
Sep. 1959	To Havana, Cuba
Dec. 1959	Returned to Myrtle Beach AFB, SC
Jan. 1960	To 4510th Combat Training Wing (TAC) Luke AFB, AZ
May 1961	To Ogden Air Material Area, Hill AFB, UT
Jul. 1962	To 2849th Air Base Wing, Hill AFB, UT
Apr. 1971	To Davis-Monthan AFB, AZ for storage
Nov. 1971	Dropped from USAF inventory
Jun. 1987	To Hill Aerospace Museum from Aero Union Corp. Chico, CA

H-21 helicopter at Hill

Sikorsky H-34J "Choctaw"

Originally designed for anti-submarine warfare in 1954, it was called by the U.S.N, "Seabat," by the Marines "Seahorse," and by the Army "Choctaw." Designed by the Sikorsky Aircraft Company of Connecticut, it was Sikorsky's most extensively built helicopter. It was widely used in Vietnam by the U.S. and 10 other nations. It is still in use throughout the world. Remarkable for its load carrying ability, it could accommodate eighteen passengers or equivalent weight in cargo. When the aircraft became outdated, it was rebuilt to extend its service life. It was suitable for day or night operation with Sikorsky auto stabilization. Notice the winch, cable, and hook above the door with which this helicopter made rescues in situations where it could not land. This aircraft was used by the 1550th ATW a tenant of HAFB.

Specifications:

Type:	General purpose transport and rescue
Crew:	2
Engine:	Wright Cyclone R-1820 of 1525 hp
Cruise:	98 mph
Rotor span:	56 ft
Length:	46 ft 9 in
Height:	15 ft 11 in
Weight:	14,000 lb.
Cost:	$425,000
Armament:	Could carry a homing torpedo externally.

Sikorsky H-34C "Choctaw" S/N 148943

Manufacturer	Sikorsky Aircraft Corp. Bridgeport, CT
Nov. 1988	Transferred to Hill AFB Museum from a display at Luke AFB, AZ

This was a Navy Aircraft and Air Force records do not exist.

Hughes OH-6 "Cayuse"

This interesting "Flying Egg" (the fuselage was 13 feet long) was submitted by Hughes in a 1963 competition for a multi-mission helicopter to include the roles of light observation, anti-submarine, photo-reconnaissance, utility transport, casualty evacuation, and light ground support. A lot of roles for one aircraft! According to a pilot who flew 3,000 hours in the "Loach" (nickname for Low Altitude Cargo Helicopter) in Vietnam, it was a great performer, it was fast, and required a minimum of maintenance. In 1966 it set 23 performance records in one month, including speed (172 mph) and altitude (28,218 ft.). By August 1970, the U.S. Army had received 1,434 of the Hughes model 500M designated as the OH-6A. It was a success commercially and also as a military export. This type aircraft was the first deployed to Grenada in October 1983. It was the first to the Persian Gulf in 1987 where it was used as an oil tanker escort. The men who flew it will always be telling stories of its daring exploits about this little gnat of a helicopter that can sting like a scorpion and disappear like a puff of smoke. This chopper was assigned to the Utah Air National Guard, and then retired from all Air National Guard duty in 1989.

Specifications:

Type:	Light observation, cargo
Crew:	2
Engine:	1 Allison T-63 turboshaft 317 shaft hp
Cruise:	132 mph; top speed 140 mph
Main rotor dia.:	27 ft 4 in
Range:	233 miles
Length:	23 ft 11 in
Weight:	2,700 lb.
Height:	8 ft 10.5 in
Total produced:	1,434
Armament:	7.62mm minigun and a 40mm grenade launcher
Cost:	N/A

Hughes 0H-6 "Cayuse" S/N 67-16132

Kaman HH-43 "Huskie"

This helicopter is especially interesting because it appears that the rotor blades would chop each other off. The fact is, they can't because the drive shaft of each rotor blade is tilted away from the other so that one rotor blade flies safely above the other. Also, the rotor blades are driven by a single transmission and are inter-meshed (synchronized) like the beaters on the mixmaster in your kitchen. This configuration first appeared in 1947 and is especially helpful in flight because one rotor cancels out the torque effect of the other eliminating the need for a tail rotor. The first production model flew in December 1958. One hundred ninety-three were subsequently ordered and assigned among all flying commands, including those in Vietnam, for fighting fires, rescue of downed pilots, and casualty evacuation. In casualty evacuation it could carry ten passengers or four litters plus a medical attendant, and a copilot. For fighting fire it carried two fully clothed firefighters equipped with 992 pounds of water and foam or compressed nitrogen. In rescue work the loudspeakers on the front were used to give directions to those being rescued. The large, ski-like floatation devices around the wheels helped prevent the helicopter from sinking if operating on a soft or snowy surface. Burma, Colombia, Morocco, Pakistan, and Iran also operated the Kaman (pronounced caw-MAN) HH-43B. This copter was the last of the so called "egg beaters." It was used for rescue and firefighting by the 1550th Aircrew Training and Test Wing at HAFB.

Specifications:

Type:	Rescue, fire fighting, casualty evacuation
Crew:	1
Engine:	Lycoming T53-L-1B of 860 shaft hp
Rotor span:	47 ft
Length:	25 ft 2 in
Height:	15 ft 6 in
Weight:	8,800 lb.
Speed:	120 mph
Cost:	N/A
Armament:	None

Kaman Aircraft Corp. HH-43 "Huskie" S/N 62-4561

Nov. 1963	Delivered to USAF by Kaman Aircraft Corp. Bloomfield, CT
Dec. 1963	To 36th Air Rescue Sq. (MATS) Tachikawa AB, Japan
Sep. 1964	Deployed to Yokota AB, Japan
Aug. 1967	To Pacific Air Rescue Center (MATS) Yokota AB, Japan
Feb. 1969	To 41st Aerospace Rescue and Recovery Wing (MATS) Yokota AB, Japan
May 1970	To 47th Aerospace Rescue and Recovery Sq. (MATS) Yokota AB, Japan
Jun. 1971	To 43rd Aerospace and Recovery Sq. (MATS) Vance AFB, OK
Sep. 1971	To 1550th Aerospace Rescue and Recovery Wing (Training) (MATS), Hill AFB, UT
Feb. 1975	To Military Aircraft Storage and Disposition Center (AF Logistics Command) Davis-Monthan AFB, AZ
Mar. 1975	Dropped from the USAF inventory by authorized reclamation
Aug. 1988	To Hill Aerospace Museum for Display

Bell HH-1H "Huey"

During 1971 the USAF received some thirty HH-1H as crash-rescue helicopter. The HH-1H featured a roof mounted rescue hoist, all weather instrumentation and tail rotor relocation to the starboard side of the tail boom. The Huey primary function was for search and rescue and support of distinguished visitors, VIPS missile sites, and range. Manufactured by Bell Helicopter Textron Inc.

Specifications:

Crew:	2
Speed:	150 mph
Length:	57 ft 3 in
Width:	9 ft 1 in
Diam. of main rotor:	48 ft
Range:	250 miles
Diam. of tail rotor:	8 ft 6 in
Armament:	2 7.62 mm machine guns
Cost:	N/A

Bell HH-1H "Huey" S/N 70-2470

Manufacturer: Bell Helicopter Textron
Date of manufacture unknown
Records of aircraft history not available.

Aircraft Engines

Allison V-1720 81/91 Inline Piston Engine

Specifications:

Manufacturer	Allison Engineering Branch, General Motors Division, Indianapolis, Indiana
Cylinders:	V-12, 1,425 hp, Right Hand Engine V1720-81
Water cooled:	With a mixture of water and Ethylene Glycol
Application:	P-38, P-40, P-51A

General Electric J-79 Turbojet

This G.E. Turbojet engine was used on several different aircraft. It was in service until the end of 1979 when it was replaced with the F100 engine made by Pratt & Whitney. 13,686 were manufactured. Hill AFB was manager for the F-4 aircraft beginning in December 1961. The F-4 used two of these engines. Date of service began in 1958.

Specifications:

Thrust:	18,730 lb. (Afterburner)
Weight:	3,847 lb.
Application:	F-16/J79 Fighting Falcon, F-4 Phantom II, B-58 Hustler, F-104 Starfighter

Pratt & Whitney R-4360 Wasp Major

For all its mass, this engine was the lightest per horsepower of any engine built at the time, .93 pounds per horsepower. Look for the main crankshaft. Around the crankshaft are four cams and seven cylinders arranged in radial fashion, for this was a radial engine called the "corncob." It was air-cooled. Seven cylinders around four crankshafts makes for twenty eight-cylinders. Each cylinder had a bore of 5.75 inches and a stroke of 6.0 inches. They're not all there now because most of them were cut away so you can see how the engine works. You'll notice they're offset. That is to maximize cooling effects as air is being forced along the outside of the engine. This gasoline fueled engine developed a maximum of 3,650 horsepower with water and alcohol fuel injection for ten minutes or less. That means each of the 28 cylinders developed about 133 horsepower each. It was fuel injected and gear-supercharged, the supercharger revolving about six times for each revolution of the crankshaft. The propeller shaft, on your right, turned once for every two revolutions of the crankshaft, being geared down by a planetary gear visible near the propeller shaft end. The revolutions of the propeller had to be slower to avoid exceeding the speed of sound at the tips, causing them to lose efficiency. The R-4360 was a very reliable engine according to pilots and mechanics. Pilots reported that the first thing mechanics did after each flight was to retighten the engine mount bolts. This remarkable engine was developed by engineers at Pratt and Whitney in 1942 using slide rules and mechanical computing machines. This engine has been in service all over the world including the Arctic and the Antarctic on the C-124 Globemaster.

Specifications:

Application: C-124, C-119, C-97, B-36, Howard Hughes' "Spruce Goose"

Pratt & Whitney R-985 Wasp "JR" Reciprocating Engine

Specifications:

Nine Cylinders Air cooled 459 Horsepower
Applications: BT-13 Vultee, C-45 Expeditor, C-2 Beaver

General Electric J-35 Turbojet

This engine was one step in the new and evolving technology of jet engines in the late 1940s. It would replace the earlier jet engines, which compressed incoming air with centrifugal force (a less efficient process). This engine has straight flow-through capabilities with eleven sets of turbine blades, each set of blades compressing the incoming air at a ratio of 4.9 to the previous set. The compression also caused the incoming air to become hot, thus making it more suitable to combustion. The straight flow-through feature made for a cleaner aerodynamic design for the aircraft. The sides of the engine have been cut away so you can see how it operates. The large disk with the single row of turbine blades on the right is turned by exhaust gases at speeds up to 24,000 rpm. The thick steel shaft in the center of the engine transfers those rpms to the eleven rows of compressor blades on the left. The compressed and heated air is mixed with JP-4 fuel. This highly volatile mixture is burned with explosive force in each of eight combustion chambers. The painted colors inside the combustion chamber indicate the colors of the JP-4 as it burns and explodes. The explosions force the engine and the aircraft forward at high speed. The exhaust gases turn the disk with the single row of turbine blades on your right and the cycle repeats itself as long as fuel is fed into the engine. Please note: It is not the exhaust gases pushing on the air behind the aircraft that force it forward. The force that pushes the aircraft forward is the explosion inside the engine. Newton described it: "To every action there is an opposite and equal reaction." General Electric built 140 of these engines. The contract was then turned over to Allison for mass production. The engines weighed 2,260 lb. and developed 5,600 lb. of thrust. We have the engine in the museum because it powered the Republic F-84G "Thunderjet" and the Northrop F-89 "Scorpion," both of which were maintained at HAFB in the late 1940s and early 1950s.

Cruise Missile Engine

Specifications:

Manufacturer:	The Williams Research Corporation
Type:	F107-WR-100 turbofan engine 600 lb. thrust
First used:	8 February 1980

Estimated total produced 3,418

A B-52 could carry 12 ALCM (AGM-88B) externally, which used this engine.

Missiles and Bombs

V-1 Vengeance Weapon "Buzzbomb"

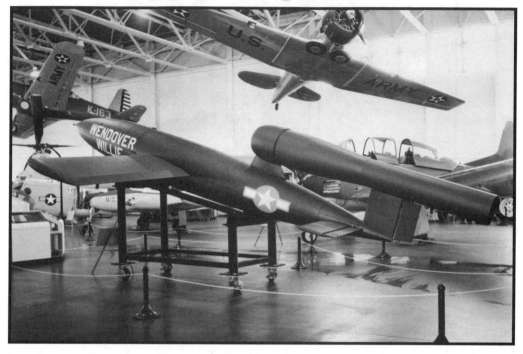

Hitler, in an effort to bring the British to their knees, drove his technicians to produce weapons like this. It was air breathing, faster than most of the Allied aircraft of WWII, and capable of flying at night in all weather, and thus it made defense against this weapon difficult for the Allies. It was launched from an inclined ramp at 220 mph. Air was admitted into the engine through a springleaf grill where it was mixed with low grade fuel and exploded driving the weapon forward. The cycle repeated itself, making the engine sound like a giant single-cylinder motorcycle. A timer reset the controls for a dive and the weapon then crashed into the approximate target area. Shooting it down was hazardous because of the debris scattered by the explosion of the high explosive warhead. Pilots of faster Allied aircraft, such as the Hawker "Tempest," sometimes slipped the wing of their own fighter under a wing of the V-1 and with a quick aileron maneuver flipped the V-1 over, upsetting the guidance system causing it to crash. The Germans first launched the weapon against England in June 1944. The RAF destroyed 1,847, but 2,340 did hit London. They launched nearly 12,000 against the Allies in Belgium. Fortunately, many crashed or were shot down before reaching the target area. The Allies captured many of them. Republic Aircraft of the United States produced this model for the armed forces; they named it the "Loon."

Specifications:

Type:	Surface-to-surface pilotless attack weapon
Cruise:	360 to 420 mph
Wingspan:	17 ft 8 in
Length:	27 ft 1 in
Weight:	4750 lb.
Height:	4 ft 8 in
Speed:	480 mph
Cost:	N/A
Produced:	N/A
Armament:	1,800 lb. conventional high explosive warhead

Boeing CIM-10 (IM-99) Bomarc "A"

The "Bomarc" was a remotely controlled unmanned interceptor. An internal target seeker took over the final guidance to the target. The CIM-10 went into production in December 1957 and become operational in 1960. The "Bomarc" was phased out in 1972. The missiles were constructed of thoristed magnesium on nearly all the surface areas. This magnesium was chosen because it offered the best combination of light weight, stiffness, and resistance to heat. (This made it strong enough to perform at temperatures encountered at over 1,500 mph.) It was also the least expensive of any of the air frame materials available.

The only difference between the A and B models are the color and the tailpipes. The A has a funnel shaped tailpipe at the compression end of the ramjet and is "black" in color.

Ogden Air Logistics Center received responsibility in 1957 and had complete logistical and managerial support of this missile.

Specifications:

Type:	Winged surface to air missile
Power plant:	THIOKOL booster of 50,000 lb. solid fuel and Two Marquardt ramjet cruise engines of 16,000 pounds each.
Wing span:	18 ft 2 in
Length:	45 ft
Diameter:	35 ft
Weight:	16,000 lb. at launch
Speed:	2,500 mph
Range:	440 miles
Warhead:	Nuclear or conventional
Service ceiling:	100,000 ft
Cost:	$555,614

Boeing CIM-10 (IM-99) Bomarc "B"

The "Bomarc" was a remotely controlled unmanned interceptor. An internal target seeker took over the final guidance to the target. The CIM-10 went into production in December 1957 and become operational in 1960. The "Bomarc" was phased out in 1972. The missiles were constructed of thoristed magnesium on nearly all the surface areas. This magnesium was chosen because it offered the best combination of light weight, stiffness, and resistance to heat. (This made it strong enough to perform at temperatures encountered at over 1,500 mph.) It was also the least expensive of any of the air frame materials available.

The only difference between the A and B models are the color and the tailpipes. The A has a funnel shaped tailpipe at the compression end of the ramjet and is "black" in color.

Ogden Air Logistics Center received responsibility in 1957 and had complete logistical and managerial support of this missile.

Specifications:

Type:	Winged surface to air missile
Power plant:	THIOKOL booster of 50,000 lb. solid fuel and Two Marquardt ramjet cruise engines of 16,000 pounds each.
Wing span:	18 ft 2 in
Length:	45 ft
Diameter:	35 ft
Weight:	16,000 lb. at launch
Speed:	2,500 mph
Range:	440 miles
Warhead:	Nuclear or conventional
Service ceiling:	100,000 ft
Cost:	$555,614

SM-62 Snark Missile

The Snark was designated as the B-62 pilotless aircraft. The Snark is a subsonic air breathing missile. It fulfilled an important role for the Strategic Air Command (SAC) as the first intercontinental guided missile. It was later replaced by the new generation of ballistic missiles. The N-69 Guidance System test missile was the first to incorporate the 24 hour Mark I guidance system. It was recoverable through the use of radio, skids, and a drag chute. Note the square enclosure over the tail cone; this contained the drag chute. Tests were started in 1953 with only 15 missiles in the system. Eight of the N-69s were successfully recovered. On 27 June 1958 the first launch of the operational prototype missile was made by Air Force personnel. Hill AFB was prime for supply and maintenance on the Snark starting in 1951 and remained prime until it was dropped from the inventory.

Specifications:

Wing Span:	42 ft
Length:	69 ft
Height:	15 ft
Weight:	60,000 lb.
Max. Speed:	mach 0.9
Cruising Speed:	mach 0.85
Service ceiling:	50,000 ft and over
Power:	(1) P&W J-57-p-17 turbojet. 10,500 lb. of thrust
Armament:	5,000 lb. warhead

Boeing LGM-30A "Minuteman"

Minuteman design began 1958 when many Americans felt intimidated by Soviet advances in rocketry that resulted in what was felt to be the "Missile Gap." This solid fuel missile changed our minds when it was successfully fired 1 February 1961. All three stages operated perfectly, sending its dummy warhead thousands of miles down range. "Wow! There goes the end of the missile gap," was heard all over the nation. It was dubbed the "Minuteman" in honor of our well-remembered Minuteman of colonial times. This type of solid fuel missile, including the improved model II, was maintained in a hardened, protective silo and could be available for instant launch. This provided a deterring third leg of the triad defensive system we Americans were building for ourselves. The other two legs being the B-52 long range bomber and the Polaris missile-launching submarines. The success of the Minuteman permitted phasing out of the liquid-fueled Atlas and Titan 1 missiles in the mid-1960s. Ogden Air Logistics Center was assigned AMA Management for the Minuteman missile in 1959.

Specifications:

Type:	Intercontinental ballistic missile.
Length:	55 ft. 9 in.
Weight:	65,000 lb. at launch.
Diameter:	6 ft.
Speed:	15,000 mph
Cost:	$1,315,000
Total produced:	Not given
Armament:	Nuclear warhead.

Boeing Semi-Trailer Transporter Erector

This unique semi-trailer is used for the transport, emplacement, and removal of the Minuteman Missile from the launching silo. The container is environmentally controlled by the tractor when on the road and by the air conditioner when stored. Towing power and emplacement/removal power is supplied by the tractor. It is also capable of transporting the missile by road or by rail. Hill AFB had major repair and upkeep for this Transporter.

Specifications:

Length:	65 ft.
Width:	10 ft 3 in
Height:	13 ft 6 in
Weight:	24,700 lb.
Cube:	8,030 ft
Cost:	$699.900

Douglas AIR-2A "Genie"

This air-to-air anti-aircraft missile was the most powerful in the world in its time because of its nuclear warhead. Designed in 1955 it was developed to protect the United States against subsonic enemy bombers. Flick-out fin-tips gave it stability and corrected for gravity drop while in flight. The process of firing the weapon is interesting. The target was tracked by Hughes MA-1, MC-10C, and MC-13 fire control systems, all from the ground. The weapon was carried aloft by the F-89 "Scorpion," F-101 "Voodoo," or F-106 "Delta Dart" aircraft. On command from the ground the weapon was armed by the pilot, ground command launched the weapon, and the aircraft immediately was maneuvered into a tight turn so as to avoid the detonation. A direct hit was unnecessary since the detonated weapon had a lethal radius of over 1,000 feet. The first live test was conducted 19 July 1957 over Yucca Flats, Nevada from an F-89J "Scorpion," like the one we have here at the Museum. Ogden Air Materiel Area was assigned as prime maintenance manager in 1956. Production of the weapon ceased in 1962. An improved TU-289 was produced in 1982.

Specifications:

Type:	Air-to-air unguided.
Fin span:	40 in.
Length:	9 ft. 7 in.
Weight:	822 lb.
Diameter:	17.5 in.
Speed:	Mach 3.3
Cost:	Not given
Total produced:	10,000+
Armament:	Nuclear 1.5 kT Warhead

McDonnell ADM-20C "Quail"

Despite its appearance as a missile, this was not an attack weapon. It was an air defense missile, air breathing, turbojet powered, to be launched from a B-52 to confuse enemy defenses and thus attract attention away from the B-52. Within its fiber glass fuselage it carried radar enhancement electronics which produced an echo that matched the radar image of the attacking B-52. A B-52 could carry four Quails in its bomb bay and had wings and tail surfaces folded down. Its guidance system was McDonnell-Summurs gyroscope and autopilot. Ogden Air Materiel Area had prime depot assignments for supply and maintenance for this missile.

Specifications:

Type:	Air defense decoy missile.
Crew:	None
Wingspan:	5 ft. 4 in.
Length:	12 ft. 10 in.
Height:	3 ft. 4 in.
Weight:	1,200 lb.
Speed:	650 mph.
Cost:	Not given
Armament:	None

Boeing AGM-86B ALCM Cruise Missile

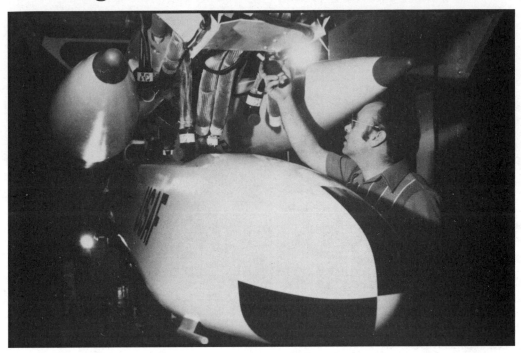

This is an early model of a cruise missile, an air-to-ground, turbofan powered, air breathing, pilotless, attack missile. It was made to be carried by the B-52G and the B-1B (which could carry eight internally and three under each wing). It could be launched hundreds of miles from the target. After launch, the wings opened from their folded position, the turbofan engine started, and it dropped to a low altitude. Able to fly under enemy radar nets, it proceeded towards its target carrying a thermonuclear warhead. An inertial guidance system directed its flight path during the first part of the flight. Overland, the TERCOM (terrain contour matching) system took over, keeping the missile within 100 feet of its planned flight path. Closely following the terrain to stay under enemy radar nets, it constantly matched the terrain pattern it "views" by radar with a map which had been stored in an on-board computer system. On its final approach to the target, last-second corrections are made with the SMAC (scene-matching area correlation) system.

Specifications:

Type:	Air-launched cruise missile.
Crew:	None
Wingspan:	12 ft.
Length:	20 ft. 9 in.
Diameter:	24.5 in.
Speed:	Mach 0.8
Weight:	2,825 lb.
Cost:	Not given
Armament:	W-80 thermonuclear warhead

Mark-5 Atomic Bomb

First production atomic bomb. Was primarily stockpiled by the US Navy, but could be carried in the bomb bay of numerous aircraft. It was about the size and shape of Fat Man that was detonated over Nagasaki, Japan on August 9, 1945. The Mark-5 used an implosion detonation method: 2,000 pounds of high explosives surrounded a ball of plutonium-239, when the explosives were detonated, the plutonium was squeezed inward, causing an uncontrolled nuclear reaction. It was years in development and served from 1948 until 1956. It was tested at Eniwetok Atoll in April and May of 1951 during Operation Greenhouse, the third US Pacific test series during which thermonuclear experiments were conducted.

Specifications:

Length:	8 ft 8.5 in.
Diameter:	4 ft 7.5 in
Weight:	3175
Yield:	40-50 Kilotons

This bomb could be used with the following aircraft: B-29, B-36, B-45, B-47, B-50, B-52

Mark-6 Atomic Bomb

MARK 6
ATOMIC BOMB

The Mark-6 was the first atomic bomb to be mass produced. It was designed to be carried in the bomb bay of an aircraft. The Mark-6 was an improvement over previous systems because it had increased yield, reduced weight, and improved aerodynamic design. The Mark-6 was extensively deployed by the USAF Strategic Air Command in the mid-1950s. SAC bombers, loaded with the Mark-6, were on alert in Europe, Africa, and the Pacific during the early days of the Cold War. It could be carried in the bomb bay of the B-29, B-36, B-47, B-50, and the B-52. The Mark-6 used the same implosion method as the Mark-5, except the Mark-6 had 3,000 pounds of high explosives surrounding the plutonium.

Specifications:

Length:	12 ft
Diameter:	6 ft 4 in
Weight:	12,000 lb.
Yield:	20-30 kilotons

Mark-7 Atomic Bomb

This Mark-7 was the first Atomic Bomb that could be carried by a fighter aircraft. It could be detonated in the air or on the ground. Notice the retractable lower fins for use on fighter aircraft.

Specifications:

Length :   15 ft 5 in
Diameter: 30 ft 5.1 in
Weight :   2000 lb.
Yield: Kiloton Range
This Bomb could be carried internally or externally.
Internally on the B-45
Externally on the F-84, F-100, F-86H, F-101

GBU-15 Guided Weapon

The USAF GBU-15 Modular Guided Weapon System is a combat proven precision guided weapon capable of destroying a variety of heavily defended targets. The GBU-15 provides tactical forces the ability to deliver either a MK-84 2,000 lb. general purpose bomb or a Blu-109/B 2,000 lb. penetrating bomb with pinpoint accuracy from low to high altitude at a significant stand off distance. It is equipped with either a television or an imaging infrared seeker. The seeker provides the launch aircraft with a visual presentation of the target and surrounding as seen from the weapon. During free flight, the presentation is transmitted by a two-way data link system to the aircraft cockpit television monitor. The seeker can be either locked onto the target before or after launch for automatic weapon guidance or it can be manually steered by the weapon-system operator.

Specifications:

Length: 154 in
Diameter: 18 in
Wing Span: 59 in
Weight: 2450 lb.
Aircraft Compatibility: F-15, F-16, F-18, F-111, F-4, B-52
Status: Operational

Rockeye II CBU-87

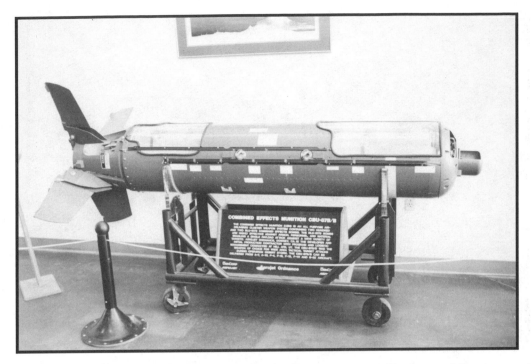

Combined Effects Munition (CEM) Description: A 1,000 lb. dispenser, opened by internal fuse or proximity sensor, operates on impact, initiating a shape-charged warhead with a fragment and incendiary ring.

Aircraft application: A7, A10, F4

Gator Mine CBU-89

A 1000 lb. dispenser opened by integral fuse or proximity sensor, mines function by trip wires or target sensing and will self-destruct at predetermined times.

Aircraft applications: A7, A10, F4

Paveway "LGB" Laser Guided Bomb

Laser guided munition consisting of a M117, 750 lb. general purpose bomb, a computer control group, and an airfoil group.

Aircraft applications: A7, A10, B52, F4, F15, F16, F111

Cluster Bomb

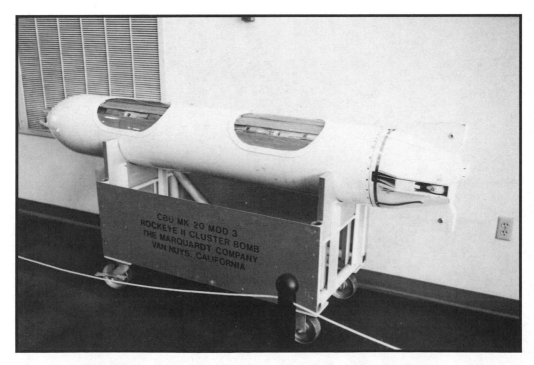

This is a cluster bomb unit (CBU) that is designed to destroy armored mechanized units to crater runways. The small shaped charges are deployed upon separation of the outer shell of the bomb unit after release from the carrying aircraft.

Aircraft applications: A7, A10, B52, F4, F15, F16, F111

Hobbs Rockwell International 2,000 lb. Bomb

Electro-optical TV guided homing 2,000 lb. bomb

Hughes AIM-4D "Falcon"

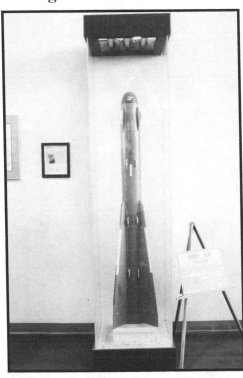

Air to air, Infra-red seek, radar guided missile, capable of low and high altitude operation and speed to mach 4, range of 6 miles. Falcon was the world's first operational guided air-to-air missile. This missile was used during the Cuban crisis. ERA: 1956-1980.

Aircraft application: F101 Voodoo

General Purpose Bomb MK-82

Description: Low drag group of bombs, 500 lb. class filled with Tritonal or H-6 Fused by nose or tail airburst. (A cluster of these bombs are hung under the F-105D Thunderchief).

Aircraft A7, A10, B52, F4, F-16, F-100, and the F-111.

General Purpose Bomb M117

Description: Thin cased Group bomb, 750 lb. class filled with 386 lb. of Tritonal or Minol. Fuses on contact. The fins on these bombs pop out upon release to slow the bombs decent so as to allow the aircraft to escape the explosion.

Hughes AGM-65 "Maverick"

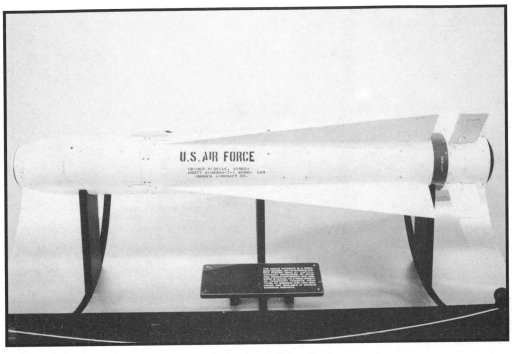

Rocket propelled, air to ground missile for use against field fortifications, SAM sites, and armored vehicles. It has a television, home on scene magnification imaging infra-red guidance system. Shaped charged warhead. Performance range: 0.6 to 14 miles.

Aircraft applications: A7, A10, F4E/G, F16, F111

Raytheon AIM-9B "Sidewinder"

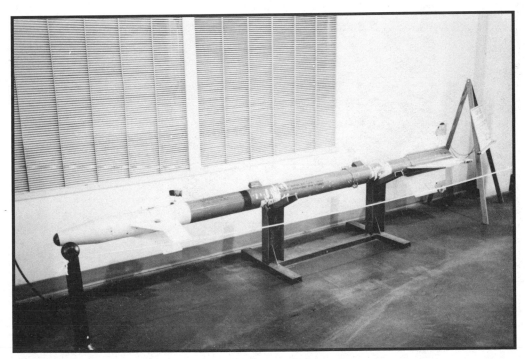

Formerly designated the GAR-8, it is a supersonic, air-to-air missile developed by the US Navy for fleet air defense and adopted by the Air Force for its F-100s, F-101s, F-105s, F-4C's. Range performance more than 10 miles at a speed of mach 2.

General Electric GAU M-61 "Avenger" 20mm Rotary Cannon

General Electric GAU M-81 "Avenger" 30mm Rotary Cannon

The Norden Bomb Sight

The Norden Bomb Sight while in service by the United States military was continually protected as a top secret piece of equipment. It always required two armed guards, or the bombardier and a crewman when transported. During a run over the target the bombardier, using set controls, piloted the aircraft by remote control until the bombs were dropped. It played a major role in Europe and against the Japanese. This bomb sight was primarily used in the B-17, B-24, B-26, and the B-29.

Cushman Scooters

On 2 April 1941 at Hill AFB a Labor, Tug, and Scooter Pool was established as a means of transporting parts, messages and other types of deliveries. This pool was to save fuel and to make it easier to get to the aircraft and other areas on base.

Landing Gear and Wheels

The world's largest landing gear
From the C-5A Galaxy

The world's smallest landing gear
From the T-38

The world's largest aircraft tire and wheel
From the Douglas B-19

Trainers

The Link trainer

B-25 trainer

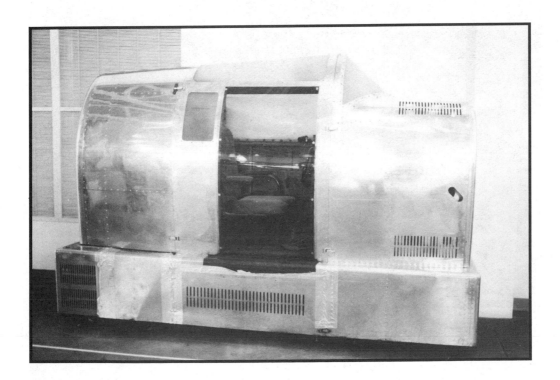

C-130 Hercules trainer

Rearview of C-130 pilot compartment (cockpit)

Miscellaneous Artifacts

Transporter GLCM M-109

This Ground Launch Cruise Missile Trailer carries four Cruise Missiles. The missiles can be fired from the trailer. TM 9-2330-365-14

Titan II ICBM Missile Nose Cone

This cone is part of the Titan II ICBM Missile. It carried a thermonuclear warhead with the largest yield of any US missile. Titan II is a two-stage ICBM which entered service in 1963 and the program was deactivated in 1987. The missile had a reaction time of one minute from it underground silo. It was 110 ft. long, 10 ft. in diameter, and had a reentry speed of approximately 17,000 mph. This cone came from the 381st Strategic Missile Wing at McConnell AFB, Kansas.

Hard Mobile Launcher (HML)

The HML consists of a manned tractor and an unmanned missile launcher, possessing both an on- and off-road capability. The launcher carries and protects the missile within a canister. On command, the canister pivots to vertical and launch-ejects the missile. On clearing the canister, the missile ignites its first stage. The launcher also contains the equipment necessary to keep the missile on alert, report operational status, and receive and execute retargeting and launch commands. The two-member crew uses the diesel-powered tractor to move the HML as directed to enlarge the area of deployment and establish launch readiness, but they do not participate in launching the missile. One significant feature of the HML is its ability to park off-road in a hardened position. When in a hardened configuration, the missile launcher is separated from the tractor. In random movement areas, the disconnected tractor can be moved nearby to assist in monitoring security.

HILL AFB WORLD WAR II CHAPEL

This restored World War II Chapel on the grounds of the Museum stands as a tribute to the faith of the military families in the times of war and peace. This non-denominational chapel in mint condition was saved from destruction through the influence of The Heritage Foundation and the efforts of many dedicated volunteers. The chapel is a key artifact in the collection at the Hill Museum. Many of our visitors were married or attended services in this chapel. Built in 1943 and in use until 1984. The chapel was moved to its present site in 1988. Local residents of the area contributed through pledges towards the restoration. It is used by appointment for weddings and special events.

Membership in the Air Force Heritage Foundation of Utah

The Air Force Heritage Foundation of Utah is a private, not-for-profit organization authorized by the State of Utah and the United States Air Force to support Hill Aerospace Museum. You can join the Foundation and help us!

The location, acquisition, and restoration of these vintage aircraft is a very expensive undertaking. Local and state financial support is sometimes available, but the bulk of our funding comes from corporations and private citizens.

Future plans for the museum include the addition of new exhibits, a Restoration Shop, Missile Park, Memorial Walk, Utah Aviation Hall of Fame Building, and a second display hangar. We need your help in achieving these goals!

Benefits for members of the Air Force Heritage Foundation of Utah include a 15% discount in the museum Gift Shop, a museum Membership Card, a subscription to our quarterly newsletter, the *Heritage Herald*, and periodic informational mailings on museum events. We invite you to join us! Just cut off the membership form below or copy it and mail it back to us. Thank you!

- -

Please check the membership category you want:

☐ Annual $10.00
☐ Sustaining Annual $25.00
☐ Contributing Annual $100.00
☐ Life $150.00
☐ Business Annual $250.00

Please mail this form and your check to:

Air Force Heritage Foundation of Utah
P.O. Box 612
Roy, Utah 84067

Name:_____

Address:_____

City, State, Zip:_____

Daytime Telephone:_____

This membership is: ☐ New   ☐ Renewal   Member No. _____